The Easy Gourmet

Summer Salads and Barbecue Cookouts

SAFEWAY

Canada Safeway Limited

EILEEN DWILLIES
ANN MERLING
ANGELA NILSEN
EDENA SHELDON

OPUS PRODUCTIONS INC.
VANCOUVER

Published and produced for Canada Safeway Limited by
Opus Productions Inc.
1128 Homer Street
Vancouver, B.C., Canada
V6B 2X6

© Copyright 1989 Opus Productions Inc.

Recipes © Copyright 1989 Eileen Dwillies, Ann Merling,
    Angela Nilsen, Edena Sheldon

Photography © Copyright 1989 Derik Murray

Canadian Cataloguing in Publication Data
    Main entry under title:
    Summer salads and barbecue cookouts

        (The Easy Gourmet ; v.2)
        Includes index.
        ISBN 0-921926-01-4

        1. Salads. 2. Barbecue cookery. I. Series.
    TX740.S84 1989   641.8'3   C89-091189-4

Corporate Consultant: Mark McCurdy, Palmer Jarvis Advertising
Editor: Mary Schendlinger
Production Manager: Orest Kinasevych
Designers: Tim Kelly, David Counsell
Recipe Coordinator: Eileen Dwillies
Food Stylist: Edena Sheldon
Test Kitchen Manager and Food Stylist Assistant: Arline Smith
Test Kitchen Staff: Marti Bjorndahl, Margot Brown, Joan Cassels,
        Fran Donis, Janet Dwillies, Betsy Filion, Arlyne Ledingham,
        Judy Lye, Jennie Meier, Joyce Miller, Marge Milne, Pat Orr,
        Barb Resvick, Alison Sclater

Produced exclusively on the IBM Personal Publishing System and
    IBM PS/2 Personal Systems.

On the cover: Perfect Grilled Steak (page 8), The Great Caesar (page 86),
Herb-Grilled Vegetables (page 37), Citrus-Spiced Sun Tea (page 146).

Printed in Canada by Friesen Printers.

"The Easy Gourmet" TM

TABLE OF CONTENTS

About the authors

Eileen Dwillies, whose recipes and articles have been published in *Western Living, Canadian Living* and other Canadian periodicals, also works as a food stylist for print and television, and teaches cooking in her home. Ann Merling is a microwave consultant, teacher and home economist whose extensive experience includes twelve years working with microwave manufacturers and teaching microwave cooking to consumers. Angela Nilsen, a home economist, food stylist and cooking instructor, has written numerous recipes and articles for publications in Europe and North America, and was a food writer with the *Vancouver Sun* for seven years. Edena Sheldon's food features and recipes have appeared in U.S. magazines, newspapers and cookbooks including *Bon Appétit, Sunset* and the *Los Angeles Times*. More recently, her work has been published in Canada, in the *Canada Cooks!* series and in *Western Living Magazine*. She enjoys a continuing reputation as a food and prop stylist.

All four authors bring to the recipes their extensive food writing experience, the unique influences of their world travels, and most of all their appreciation of the cooking traditions of Western Canada, where all of them make their home.

About the recipes

Every recipe in this book is carefully and thoroughly kitchen-tested, by a team that includes both new and experienced cooks.

For convenience in shopping and measuring, we "rounded off" in listing the metric quantities of recipe ingredients; 1 lb. is converted as 500 g, rather than the technically correct 454 g; 1/2 lb. is shown as 250 g, and so on.

All of the microwave recipes were tested in microwave ovens of 700 watts, so if yours is in the 600 watt range, add 15% to the suggested cooking times. And remember to start with the minimum suggested time and add extra if necessary—every microwave, like every convection oven, is unique.

The heat and cooking times shown in the barbecue recipes are applicable to any kind of barbecue. In kitchen-testing, we used a gas barbecue.

We used large eggs and whole milk unless specified otherwise, and we used unsalted butter without exception. When you cook with herbs, remember that dried herbs are much more concentrated than fresh ones, so if you substitute dried herbs for fresh, use one-third the amount. When a recipe calls for wine, liqueur, or other alcoholic beverage, there is usually a substitute ingredient listed. There are non-alcoholic cooking wines and liqueurs available, but unless the recipe specifically calls for them, we did not use them, as their salt content is quite high.

Please note: In the process of preparing this second volume of *The Easy Gourmet*, our cookbook team has updated Volume One (*Entrées; The Main Event*). These notes appear on page 160 of this book. Between now and then, have a delicious summer!

INTRODUCTION

Welcome to *The Easy Gourmet: Summer Salads and Barbecue Cookouts*, the second in a series of four cookbooks created this year to celebrate Canada Safeway's Sixtieth Anniversary.

Everyone loves the taste of summer — a sizzling steak right off the hot coals, a refreshing salad of colourful summer vegetables, tangy-sweet desserts and coolers made from fresh summer fruits. In this book, the four top food writers who created the inspiring main dish recipes in our first volume, *Entrées: The Main Event*, have gone all out to bring you the best in summer eating. Look through these pages and you'll find recipes that make memorable warm weather meals. Every recipe has been carefully kitchen-tested, and all of them take advantage of the cornucopia of fresh foods available in Safeway stores throughout the summer months, as well as the convenience foods that leave you lots of time for your summer visitors. And remember, all of the specialty departments at Safeway are staffed by fully trained and experienced personnel. Need advice or information? Ask the experts!

Some of the recipes in this volume are designed for preparation in the microwave (a real friend to the summer cook!). Look for the special microwave symbol ⓜ .

So celebrate our Sixtieth with us — get out your barbecue, invite your friends, and try these tantalizing original recipes, from old favourites like Barbecued Lamb Chops with Tsatziki Sauce and The Great Caesar Salad to wonderful new ideas like Grilled Monkfish with Lime Butter and Persian Cucumber Salad. Summer has never tasted better!

The Barbecue

The cookout recipes in *The Easy Gourmet* can be prepared on any type of barbecue, from the simplest charcoal-burning hibachi to the most sophisticated gas grill. Here are some tips on selecting and using the perfect one for you.

The Open Brazier, the "grand-daddy of grills," is an uncovered grill, sometimes equipped with a hood. The table-top hibachi is in this category. Choose one with an adjustable grill so that you can control the heat.

The Covered Barbecue is a rounded, two-piece grill also known as the "kettle." It has legs or wheels, comes in a variety of sizes, and has dampers on the lid and firebox to regulate heat and air flow. Uncovered, it works like an open brazier; covered, it is more like an oven and can handle whole roasts and fish.

The Grill Wagon is a deluxe appliance for the serious chef. It is covered and can be moved easily on its large wheels. Common accessories include carving boards, rotisserie spits, elevated warming shelves, swing-up work surfaces and a system of dampers and vents that allows the cook to fine-tune the air and heat levels. The heavy fitted lid makes the very most of aromatic woods and herbs.

The Gas Barbecue is a dependable, convenient grill that provides the right temperature at the right time, with no fuss and very little clean-up. Natural gas units must be connected permanently to a gas line, and propane units come with bottled gas which makes them more portable. Ceramic "coals" are heated by the gas flames, creating a great barbecue flavour that is quickly becoming a new favourite.

The Heat

Hot coals are partially covered with grey ash. *Medium-Hot* coals glow red through a layer of grey ash. *Low* coals are completely covered with ash and no glow can be seen.

Changing the temperature of a gas barbecue is as easy as turning the control knob. For non-gas barbecues, raise the temperature by pushing the coals closer together and knocking away some of the ash. Fan them with a folded-up newspaper until they glow. Or simply lower the grill so it is closer to the heat source. To lower the temperature, separate the coals into a single layer with spaces between the coals. Raise the grill, or mist with water.

The Tools

Tongs. A must for turning meat and poultry—if you use a fork, some of the juices will escape.

Metal Pancake Turner. Use a flat one without holes for turning fish, vegetables, and fruits.

Pot Holder and Mitts. Heavy-duty, and non-flammable.

Meat Thermometer. The new, slender, "instant-reading" types are terrific for testing the internal heat of grilled meats. Insert them in the thickest part of the meat.

Basting Brushes. The single most important tool, because of all those wonderful sauces and marinades that give the food its special summer flavour. They should have long handles. You'll want both the fine-bristled ones (for smaller items) and the wide, paintbrush types for larger poultry. Wash them well and dry completely between uses, and they will last a long time.

Water Spritzer. For those quick flare-ups caused by dripping fats and juices.

Bib Apron with Pockets. And tuck a tea towel into your belt or pocket. It's convenient for hand-wiping—something you'll be doing a lot of.

Hinged Wire Basket. The type that opens up like a book is great for holding burgers, smaller fish, shrimp, chops, and chicken wings.

Skewers. The long metal ones, for meats and kebabs; shorter metal and wooden ones for appetizers and smaller portions. Soak wooden ones in water for 15-20 minutes before using, and they won't burn during the cooking.

Wire Brush. To clean the grill between uses—essential for good barbecue results. Use the steel plate on top of the brush to scrape off tough char, and the bristles to clean the rack. Hold it under very hot running water to clean it, and shake it dry to prevent rusting.

The Fuel

Charcoal is the classic, and it's now available in hardwoods. Oak and hickory charcoal produce aromatic, flavourful smoke. Aromatic woods such as cherry and alder don't burn as hot as charcoal but they give a subtle smokey flavour. Mesquite gives an intense smokey taste and burns sizzling hot. Oak gives a medium smokey flavour to burgers, chicken, fish and lamb. Use applewood for a sweet, nutty flavour in chicken, seafood, ham, bacon and sausages. You can use chips of these woods right in the charcoal—just soak them in warm water and toss them on the hot coals.

The Cooking Time

Cooking times and heat levels are given in every barbecue recipe in these pages. To test meat, fish or poultry for doneness, just press your index finger into the cooked meat. *Rare* meat will feel soft, almost squishy, and hardly any indentation will be left. *Medium-Rare* meat will be springy, with some give but some resistance. *Well-Done* meat will be very firm to the touch. In many of the recipes for barbecued meats, we suggest letting the meat "rest" for a few minutes before carving or serving. This allows the juices to re-absorb, and makes carving easier.

The Salads

Up-to-date storage and transportation methods mean that a great variety of fresh foods can be had at Safeway all year round, but one of the best things about summer is the truly beautiful array of fresh local produce that perks up any meal of any day. *The Easy Gourmet* is chock-full of recipes for light summertime salads, to accompany more hearty main dishes, or to be served on their own on hot summer evenings, or for special luncheons on the patio. Try Kiwi Chicken Salad for a nourishing, refreshing main dish on a warm night, Mexican Fiesta Taco Salad when you have a house full of kids, Potato Pesto Salad or Asparagus with Tomato Vinaigrette to complete the menu at a summer cookout.

Summer Complements

This volume of *The Easy Gourmet* winds up with a special section on summer complements: refreshing soups, quick and tasty sandwiches, cooling beverages and melt-in-your-mouth desserts that will round out any warm weather dinner. Bring out a pitcher of icy-cool Citrus-Spiced Sun Tea to enjoy while the coals are heating, serve Chilled Minestrone with Pesto as a starter, top off your barbecue with a crowd-pleasing Glazed Fruit Flan. At this time of year Safeway's produce department is bursting with the colours and flavours of summer, so take advantage, and enjoy!

BARBECUES

In this section, you'll find tantalizing main-dish cookout recipes that take advantage of the wide variety of meat, poultry and seafood available at Safeway stores: try Hickory-Smoked Chicken Quarters, Perfect Grilled Steak or the classic Pacific Stuffed Salmon. Sweet-and-Sour Fruit Kebabs or Herb-Grilled Vegetables make wonderful accompaniments—barbecue them right alongside the entrée to complete your hot-off-the-grill feast.

PERFECT GRILLED STEAK

One of the best steaks to be had is done the Florentine way in Italy — briefly marinated with olive oil, thyme and rosemary, and seared quickly over hot charcoal. Crusty on the outside and rosy red on the inside, carved into thick slices and served with this savoury skillet sauce, this is a steak to reckon with! Serve it with a heap of fresh steak fries and crisp watercress. The Great Caesar salad (p. 86) is the perfect accompaniment. Serves 4-6.

2	Porterhouse or T-bone steaks, each about 1 1/2 - 2 lbs. (750 g-1 kg), 2 inches (5 cm) thick	2
1/2 cup	extra virgin olive oil	125 mL
2 tbsp.	cracked black peppercorns	30 mL
2 tbsp.	dried rosemary, *or*	30 mL
6 tbsp.	fresh rosemary	90 mL
2 tbsp.	dried thyme, *or*	30 mL
4 tbsp.	fresh thyme	60 mL
	salt to taste	
	Savoury Skillet Sauce (recipe follows)	

Bring the steaks to room temperature. Brush with olive oil on both sides, sprinkle with the pepper, rosemary and thyme, and allow to marinate at room temperature for about 45 minutes.

Meanwhile, heat the barbecue to hot. Lightly oil the grill and sear the steaks 4-6 inches (10-15 cm) above the heat source, for 5-7 minutes per side to seal in juices. Turn the steaks with tongs, and sear the other side. Continue to grill steaks to rare or medium-rare, with a total cooking time of about 15 minutes. To test the meat, press it with your finger: the meat should just begin to feel resistant to the touch. Season the steaks with salt on both sides during the final moments of grilling.

Remove the steaks from the grill. Allow the steaks to rest on a carving board 4-5 minutes before carving. Using a very sharp, thin-bladed knife, cut the meaty portions from the bone. Carve the meat into 1 inch (2.5 cm) wide slices, and serve at once. Spoon 1-2 generous spoonfuls of Savoury Skillet Sauce over each portion.

SAVOURY SKILLET SAUCE

6 tbsp.	butter	90 mL
2 tbsp.	olive oil	30 mL
1/2 cup	minced shallots	125 mL
1	clove garlic, crushed	1
1 tbsp.	dried rosemary, crumbled, *or*	15 mL
3 tbsp.	fresh rosemary	45 mL
1 tsp.	dried thyme, crumbled, *or*	5 mL
1 tbsp.	fresh thyme	15 mL
1 tbsp.	Worcestershire sauce	15 mL
2 tbsp.	fresh lemon juice	30 mL
1/2 cup	whipping cream	125 mL
1 tbsp.	Dijon mustard	15 mL
2 tbsp.	green peppercorns, drained	30 mL
	salt and pepper to taste	

Heat the butter and oil in a heavy skillet until bubbly. Add the shallots and garlic, and quickly sauté 3-5 minutes until softened. Stir in the rosemary, thyme, Worcestershire sauce and lemon juice. Heat until bubbly, 2 minutes. Add the cream, and cook the sauce over medium-high heat several minutes until slightly thickened and bubbly. The sauce should just coat a spoon. Finally, reduce the heat, whisk in the mustard and peppercorns, and heat 1 minute to warm through. Remove from heat, and season to taste with salt and pepper. Serve over steak.

The Easy Gourmet features a photograph of this recipe on the front cover.

CAJUN-STYLE STEAK

Most Creole and Cajun recipes use a mixture of seasonings that vary only slightly according to the whim of the chef. The mixture is made up ahead of time and added as needed instead of salt and pepper. This is one variation — change it according to your tastes, pack it into a spice jar and keep it in the refrigerator until you need it. Pressed into the sides of a thick T-bone steak and quickly grilled, it will wake up your taste buds! Serve some cooling Citrus Fruit Dip (p. 123) while the meat is cooking and present the steak with baked potatoes and all the trimmings. Serves 4.

4	1 1/2-2 inch (3.5-5 cm) thick	4
	T-bone or steaks of your choice	
	Cajun Seasoning (recipe follows)	

Liberally press Cajun Seasoning into the sides of the meat. Heat the barbecue to hot and sear the meat on both sides to blacken. Reduce the heat and broil until done, about 5 minutes each side for rare, and serve.

CAJUN SEASONING

1 tbsp.	salt	15 mL
1 tbsp.	paprika	15 mL
3/4 tsp.	cayenne pepper	3 mL
1/2 tsp.	white pepper	2 mL
1/2 tsp.	black pepper	2 mL
1/2 tsp.	dry mustard	2 mL
1/4 tsp.	dried oregano *or*	1 mL
1 tsp.	finely chopped fresh oregano	5 mL
1/4 tsp.	dried thyme *or*	1 mL
1 tsp.	finely minced fresh thyme	5 mL
pinch	crushed dried bay leaf	pinch

Mix all ingredients together and store in the refrigerator or freezer.

PEPPERED FILLET OF BEEF

The tenderest of all steaks, the tenderloin of beef, is all meat. Serve this variation of a peppercorn steak with sizzling pan-fried mushrooms and ranch cut potatoes. For added flavour, add soaked wood chips, such as hickory, apple, oak or cherry, to the coals. Serves 2-3.

1/3 cup	whole black peppercorns	75 mL
1	whole beef tenderloin, about 1 - 1 1/4 lbs. (500-625 g)	1
1 cup	whipping cream	250 mL
1 tsp.	Dijon mustard or to taste	5 mL
1 tsp.	Worcestershire sauce	5 mL
4-6	thick slices of baguette bread, lightly toasted	4-6

Place the whole peppercorns between two sheets of waxed paper and coarsely crush with a rolling pin. Generously press crushed peppercorns over the tenderloin. Refrigerate until ready to cook.

Heat the barbecue to medium or medium-hot and place the meat on an oiled grill. Cook, turning once, about 12-15 minutes on each side or until a meat thermometer registers 125°F (50°C) for rare, 140°F (60°C) for medium. Brush off excess peppercorns and place the meat on a carving board. For easier carving, allow the meat to stand for 10 minutes.

Meanwhile, in a medium saucepan, bring the cream to a rapid boil. Watch carefully as it will overflow easily. Reduce the heat and boil until reduced by half. Stir in the mustard and Worcestershire Sauce.

Place two toasted rounds of baguette on each serving plate. Slice the meat thinly or into 4-6 thick pieces and place on top of the bread. Stir meat juices into the sauce and pour over each serving.

MEXICAN BEEF ROLLS

*The lively, unusual blend of herbs and spices in this marinade make it quite
versatile, so you can use it on other cuts of meat such as whole sirloin steaks.
Make sure you soak the skewers in water first before threading on the meat,
so they do not burn on the barbecue. To complete your Mexican theme dinner,
serve saffron rice and a tomato and onion salad. Serves 4.*

4 tbsp.	vegetable oil	60 mL
1	shallot, very finely chopped	1
1	clove garlic, crushed	1
1 1/2 tbsp.	red wine vinegar	20 mL
1 tbsp.	fresh lime juice	15 mL
1 tbsp.	chili powder	15 mL
1 tsp.	ground cumin	5 mL
1/2 tsp.	dried oregano	2 mL
1/4 tsp.	cinnamon	1 mL
1/4 tsp.	*each* salt and pepper	1 mL
1 lb.	beef top sirloin steak, 3/4 - 1 inch	500 g
	(1.5-2.5 cm) thick, trimmed	
12	mushroom caps	12
4	wooden skewers, 12 inches (30 cm) long,	4
	soaked in water for 20 minutes	
1	small yellow bell pepper, cored, seeded and	1
	cut into 12 squares	
	chopped fresh parsley for garnish	

Heat the oil in a small saucepan and add the shallot and garlic. Cook until
the shallot is soft. Stir in the vinegar, lime juice, chili powder, cumin,
oregano, cinnamon, salt and pepper. Simmer, covered, for 5 minutes. Cool.

Cut the beef into 12 cubes, 1 1/2 - 2 inches (4-5 cm) square. Place between 2
sheets of waxed paper and beat with a meat mallet or rolling pin into thin
pieces about 5 x 2 1/2 inches (13 x 6 cm). Place a mushroom in the centre of
each piece of meat and roll up the beef. Secure with toothpicks. Place the
beef in a single layer in a shallow dish. Pour the cooled marinade over the
meat. Cover and marinate in the refrigerator, turning occasionally.

Heat the barbecue to medium-hot. Remove the toothpicks and thread 3 pieces of beef onto each skewer alternating with 3 pieces of pepper. Brush the grill with oil and cook the beef rolls for 10-15 minutes or until cooked, turning once. Place the meat on a serving platter, garnish with chopped parsley, and serve.

G REAT CANADIAN CHEESEBURGERS

Kids and grown-ups alike just love to tuck into a thick, juicy burger — and what's better for a backyard barbecue? Serve them with your favourite deli potato salad, pickles, and a pitcher of Old-Fashioned Lemon-Limeade (p. 147). Serves 4.

1 lb.	regular ground beef	500 g
1 cup	grated sharp Cheddar cheese	250 mL
1	medium onion, finely chopped	1
1 tbsp.	dried oregano, crumbled	15 mL
1 tbsp.	Worcestershire sauce	15 mL
1/2 tsp.	freshly ground black pepper	2 mL
1/2 tsp.	salt	2 mL
4	slices tomato	4
4	slices sharp Cheddar cheese, each 2 1/2 inches (6 cm) square	4
4	hamburger buns	4
	assorted mustards and relishes	
	sliced tomatoes, thinly sliced red onion, leaf lettuce, thinly sliced dill pickles and avocado	

In a large bowl, combine thoroughly but lightly the ground beef, grated Cheddar, onion, oregano, Worcestershire sauce, pepper and salt. Shape the mixture into four 4 inch (10 cm) patties. Cover and refrigerate 1 hour. Heat the barbecue to hot. Grill the burgers about 8 minutes per side or until cooked as desired. Place 1 slice of tomato and 1 slice of cheese on top of each burger and cook an additional 2-3 minutes or until the cheese begins to melt. Toast the hamburger buns lightly on the edges of the grill until golden. Tuck the finished burgers into the toasted buns and serve at once with a platter of condiments.

The Easy Gourmet features a photograph of this recipe on page 17.

S MOKIES WITH MUSTARD BUTTER

No one can resist these embellished hot dogs! Big Bavarian-style smokies are wrapped "candy-cane" fashion with bacon, grilled until crisp and sizzling, then tucked into toasted buns with a savoury mustard-spiked butter and thinly sliced onion and tomato. Serve with deli cole slaw, crisp potato chips, and big deli pickles. Makes 12.

12	natural casing Bavarian smokies	12
	(about 2 lbs. (1 kg))	
12	slices bacon (1/2 lb. (250 g)), at room temperature	12
12	sesame-seed topped frankfurter buns	12
	or small "hero" buns	
	Grainy Mustard Butter (recipe follows)	
	sliced tomatoes	
	thinly sliced purple onion	

Heat the barbecue to medium-hot. Cut shallow diagonal slashes on both sides of each smokie. Wrap 1 slice of bacon around each smokie, "candy-cane" fashion, securing the ends with wooden toothpicks. Grill 6 inches (15 cm) above the heat source, turning frequently, until the smokies are sizzling hot and the bacon is crisp and golden brown, about 20 minutes. While the franks are grilling, toast the insides of each bun, opened up flat, to a golden brown and spread with Grainy Mustard Butter. Tuck in the smokies, add slices of tomato and onion, and serve at once.

GRAINY MUSTARD BUTTER

Prepare this butter up to 1 week before serving, stored tightly capped and refrigerated. Let soften before spreading.

1/2 lb.	softened butter	250 g
1/3 cup	finely minced fresh parsley	75 mL
3 tbsp.	*each* sweet grainy German-	45 mL
	style mustard and Dijon mustard	
2 tbsp.	honey	30 mL
1 tbsp.	cider vinegar	15 mL

14

Using a food processor, cream together all ingredients until fluffy and well blended. Store in a tightly sealed crock, refrigerated, until ready to serve.

The Easy Gourmet features a photograph of this recipe on page 17.

ONEY-MINT LAMB CHOPS

Lamb and mint are just made for each other, and combined with a lime and honey marinade, they are a superb combination. Watch the chops carefully as they barbecue so the honey does not burn. Tiny new potatoes and fresh peas make perfect accompaniments. Serves 4.

4	sirloin lamb chops, about 1 inch (2.5 cm) thick, about 1 1/2 lbs. (750 g)	4
Honey-Mint Marinade:		
4 tbsp.	honey	60 mL
4 tbsp.	vegetable oil	60 mL
1	large clove garlic, crushed	1
1 tbsp.	fresh lime juice	15 mL
1 tbsp.	chopped fresh mint	15 mL
1 1/2 tsp.	dry mustard	7 mL
1/4 tsp.	*each* salt and pepper	1 mL
	fresh mint leaves for garnish	

Place the lamb chops in a shallow dish. To make the marinade, in a measuring jug or small bowl, combine the honey, oil, garlic, lime juice, mint, mustard, salt and pepper, stirring until well mixed.

Pour the marinade over the lamb, turning to coat. Cover and marinate in the refrigerator for 2-3 hours, turning occasionally.

Heat the barbecue to medium-hot. Place the chops on the grill and cook 5 minutes to sear the meat. Reduce the heat to medium-low and cook a further 10-12 minutes, turning and brushing occasionally with the marinade. Watch carefully so the marinade does not burn. Serve on a warm platter garnished with mint leaves.

HERB-GARLIC LEG OF LAMB

When summer entertaining heralds a special event, a luxurious butterflied leg of lamb makes superb fare. The nice bonus is that the thicker portions provide rare slices, and the thinner edge portions provide crustier, medium-done slices. Serve with creamy scalloped potatoes, fresh green beans in a herb-flecked vinaigrette and sliced beefsteak tomatoes. Serves 6-8.

2/3 cup	olive oil	150 mL
1/3 cup	dry red wine	75 mL
6	cloves garlic, crushed	6
2 tbsp.	Dijon mustard	30 mL
3 tbsp.	*each* snipped fresh rosemary and thyme	45 mL
2 tsp.	cracked black pepper	10 mL
2 tsp.	salt	10 mL
2 tbsp.	honey or molasses	30 mL
1	4 lb. (2 kg) leg of lamb, boned and butterflied	1
	sprigs of fresh rosemary and thyme for garnish	

Whisk together the olive oil, red wine, garlic, mustard, rosemary, thyme, pepper, salt and honey. Press the lamb out flat in a large, shallow dish. Brush the marinade over both sides, turning the lamb once to coat evenly. Allow the lamb to marinate 2-3 hours in the refrigerator, loosely covered with waxed paper.

Heat the barbecue to medium-hot. Lightly oil the grill. While the barbecue is heating, bring the lamb to room temperature.

Place the lamb on the grill, 4-6 inches (10-15 cm) above the heat source, fat side down, and sear 12 minutes. Turn the lamb over and sear an additional 12 minutes, brushing with marinade. Turn the lamb, and continue to baste and grill for a total cooking time of 35-45 minutes, 10 minutes more for medium. The internal temperature should be 140°F (60-65°C) on an instant-read thermometer inserted into thickest portion; this will result in medium-rare with medium outer portions. Season with salt and pepper on both sides during the final minutes.

Let the lamb rest on a carving board 10-12 minutes before carving to allow the juices to absorb. Garnish with sprigs of rosemary and thyme.

Opposite: (Left to right) Smokies with Mustard Butter (page 14) and Great Canadian Cheeseburgers (page 13).

PARTY SOUVLAKI

Souvlaki — barbecued marinated lamb kebabs — make great summer entertaining fare. The tantalizing aroma of the grilling meat whets everyone's appetite and invites seconds and thirds! Serve with Zorba The Greek Salad (p. 94), a platter of hummus, chilled stuffed vine leaves and warm pita breads done on the grill with a brush of olive oil. Serves 6-8.

1 1/2 cups	olive oil	375 mL
3	cloves garlic, crushed	3
1/3 cup	fresh lemon juice	75 mL
1/4 cup	red wine vinegar	50 mL
2 tbsp.	*each* dried oregano and mint, crumbled	30 mL
1 tsp.	ground cumin	5 mL
1/2 tsp.	allspice	2 mL
1 tsp.	coarsely ground black pepper	5 mL
3 lbs.	boneless lamb, cut from the leg,	1.5 kg
	cut into 1 inch (2.5 cm) chunks	
	salt to taste	
	Tsatziki Sauce (p. 22)	
	lemon wedges and sprigs of fresh mint for garnish	

Whisk together the olive oil, garlic, lemon juice, vinegar, oregano, mint, cumin, allspice and pepper. Pour over the chunks of lamb, toss gently to coat evenly, cover and marinate overnight, chilled.

Heat the barbecue to hot. While the coals are heating, bring the lamb to room temperature. Thread the lamb on skewers and brush with marinade. Lightly oil the grill and cook the lamb 4 inches (10 cm) above the heat source, turning once or twice and brushing with the marinade, until crusty on the outside and rosy pink and juicy on the inside, about 10 minutes total. Salt to taste.

Remove the skewers from the grill. Brush the pitas with a light film of olive oil on both sides. Place on the edges of the grill, and lightly toast until very pale golden and warmed through. Serve the lamb kebabs hot, garnished with lemon wedges and mint and accompanied by the chilled Tsatziki Sauce and warmed pita breads.

G IANT LAMB KEBABS WITH SPICY TOMATO BUTTER

Savoury, succulent lamb kebabs team up with skewers of colourful vegetables in this hearty cookout dinner. While everything is still sizzling hot, add a drizzle of tomato-spiked butter, then serve it all up with roasted potatoes, a crisp green salad, and a crusty loaf of French bread. Serves 4.

1/3 cup	olive oil	75 mL
2 tbsp.	*each* fresh lemon juice, orange juice and red wine vinegar	30 mL
2	bay leaves, crumbled	2
1 tbsp.	*each* dried oregano, thyme and rosemary, crumbled	15 mL
3 tbsp.	soy sauce	45 mL
1 tsp.	cracked black pepper	5 mL
2 lbs.	boneless lamb, cut from the leg, cut into 1 1/2 inch (3.5 cm) cubes	1 kg
16	cherry tomatoes	16
2	red onions cut into 1 inch (2.5 cm) pieces	2
3	green bell peppers, cut into 1 inch (2.5 cm) squares	3
3	zucchini, split lengthwise and cut in 1 1/2 inch (3.5 cm) cubes	3
12	large mushroom caps	12
3	Japanese eggplants, cut crosswise into 1 1/2 inch (3.5 cm) pieces	3
	olive oil	
	salt to taste	
	Spicy Tomato Butter (recipe follows)	

Whisk together the oil, lemon and orange juices, vinegar, bay leaves, oregano, thyme, rosemary, soy sauce and pepper. Pour the mixture over the lamb cubes, toss to coat, and refrigerate 6 hours, turning the meat several times as it marinates.

Thread the vegetables on long skewers and brush with oil. Remove the meat from the marinade, drain (reserve the marinade), and thread on skewers.

Heat the barbecue to medium-hot. Oil the grill and cook the lamb and vegetables 4-6 inches (10-15 cm) above the heat source, turning and basting with the reserved marinade. Grill until the meat is medium to medium-rare, about 10-15 minutes, and the vegetables are just tender and golden brown. Season the meat with salt before removing it from the grill.

With a long-tined fork, push the lamb from the skewers onto a large warm platter. Surround the meat with the vegetables, and drizzle everything with Spicy Tomato Butter before serving.

SPICY TOMATO BUTTER

1/2 cup	finely minced onion	125 mL
2 tbsp.	*each* fresh orange juice and red wine vinegar	30 mL
1/2 tsp.	*each* chili powder and dried thyme	2 mL
3 tbsp.	tomato paste	45 mL
1 tbsp.	brown sugar, packed	15 mL
1 cup	melted butter	250 mL

Combine the onion, orange juice, vinegar, chili powder and thyme in a small saucepan. Simmer over medium heat until 2 tbsp. (30 mL) of liquid remains. The mixture should be syrupy and the onions soft and translucent. Set aside until just barely warm.

In a food processor or blender, purée the onion mixture. Add the tomato paste and brown sugar, and blend smooth. With the motor running, add the melted butter in a slow, steady stream.

Drizzle the butter warm over the hot grilled lamb and vegetables just before serving.

The Easy Gourmet features a photograph of this recipe on page 71.

BARBECUED LAMB CHOPS WITH TSATZIKI SAUCE

Nothing is quite as delicate and delicious as loin lamb chops cut thick and grilled over hot coals. Perfect accompaniments are grilled eggplant wedges and split zucchini, a hot rice pilaf, Greek olives and fresh tomatoes drizzled with olive oil. Serves 4.

1/3 cup	olive oil	75 mL
3 tbsp.	fresh lemon juice	45 mL
	grated rind of 1 lemon	
2 tbsp.	*each* dried oregano and mint leaves, crumbled	30 mL
1	small red onion, minced	1
1 tsp.	*each* salt and pepper	5 mL
8	loin lamb chops, each 1 1/2 inches (3.5 cm) thick	8
	Tsatziki Sauce (recipe follows)	

Whisk together the oil, lemon juice and rind, oregano, mint, onion, salt and pepper until smooth. Brush the marinade over both sides of the chops, and marinate in a cool place 1-2 hours. Heat the barbecue to hot. Lightly oil the grill and sear the meat 4 inches (10 cm) above the heat source for 4-5 minutes per side, brushing with marinade after searing. Grill until the chops are a rich golden brown on both sides, medium-rare on the inside. To test, press the chops with your finger: the meat should feel just slightly firm. Total cooking time will be about 14-16 minutes.

TSATZIKI SAUCE

2 cups	plain yogourt, whisked smooth	500 mL
1 cup	grated, peeled long English cucumber	250 mL
2	small cloves garlic, crushed	2
1/2 tsp.	salt	2 mL
pinch	white pepper	pinch
2 tbsp.	dried mint leaves, crumbled	30 mL
2 tbsp.	finely minced fresh parsley	30 mL

Combine all ingredients. Cover and chill 3-4 hours to blend the flavours. Serve cool as an accompaniment to the grilled lamb chops.

PROVENCAL BARBECUED RACK OF LAMB

Mention rack of lamb and everyone's mouth seems to water. In this recipe, it is marinated briefly in a zesty herb-mustard mixture, then grilled to a succulent crusty turn. Serve with hot buttered orzo sprinkled with Parmesan, and grilled fresh zucchini. Serves 4.

4	individual racks of lamb	4
	(6-7 chops each)	
1/2 cup	olive oil	125 mL
3	large cloves garlic, crushed	3
1 tbsp.	*each* dried rosemary, oregano, thyme,	15 mL
	basil and savoury	
4 tbsp.	Dijon mustard	60 mL
2 tbsp.	*each* fresh lemon juice	30 mL
	and red wine vinegar	
	grated rind of 1 lemon	
2	bunches fresh rosemary	2
	salt and pepper to taste	

Clean and trim the racks of lamb, and wipe with a wet cloth. Whisk together the olive oil, garlic, herbs, mustard, lemon juice, vinegar and lemon rind. Brush the marinade over the lamb on both sides, and allow to sit at room temperature 2 hours on a shallow tray or platter in a single layer, fat side up (this helps the marinade to adhere). Meanwhile, soak the bunches of rosemary in cold water.

Heat the barbecue to hot. Drain the rosemary, and scatter directly over the coals. Lightly oil the grill and place the lamb on it, thickest side down, 4 inches (10 cm) above the heat source. Sear 5-6 minutes, then turn and sear the other side. Continue to grill for a total cooking time of about 18 minutes, basting with any additional marinade, until crusty on the outside, and rosy pink on the inside. The internal temperature should be 140°F (60-65°C) on an instant-read thermometer for medium-rare. Season with salt and pepper during the final 2 minutes.

Let the lamb rest 7-8 minutes before carving. Serve 1 rack per portion, with steak knives for carving each rib into finger-held "chops."

LAMB BURGERS WITH FRESH MINT CHUTNEY

Try these savoury, fragrantly-spiced lamb burgers done up over hot coals so they're crisp on the outside, juicy on the inside. Tuck them into warm pita breads and drizzle with Fresh Mint Chutney. A basket of bright cherry tomatoes, cucumber spears, and a cold rice salad make perfect go-withs. Serves 6.

	Fresh Mint Chutney (recipe follows)	
2 lbs.	lean ground lamb	1 kg
2	cloves garlic, minced	2
1	medium onion, chopped	1
1	small green bell pepper, seeded and stemmed	1
2 tbsp.	*each* fresh lemon juice and grated lemon rind	30 mL
2	eggs, lightly beaten	2
1/3 cup	*each* toasted pine nuts and dried currants (if currants are not plump, soak 5 minutes in warm water and drain)	75 mL
2 tsp.	*each* salt, dried oregano and dried basil	10 mL
1 tsp.	*each* ground black pepper and cumin	5 mL
2 tbsp.	fine dry bread crumbs	30 mL

Prepare the Fresh Mint Chutney several hours before serving for the best flavour.

Place the lamb in a large mixing bowl. In a food processor, grind together the garlic, onion and bell pepper until finely minced. Add to the lamb, and combine with the lemon juice, lemon rind, eggs, pine nuts, currants, salt, oregano, basil, pepper, cumin and bread crumbs. Mix thoroughly but gently, using a fork or an electric mixer fitted with a dough hook.

With moistened hands, shape the mixture into 6 generous 4 inch (10 cm) patties, each about 1 inch (2.5 cm) thick. Place the burgers on a flat tray or platter, cover loosely with waxed paper, and refrigerate 4 hours to allow the flavours to blend before grilling.

Heat the barbecue to medium-hot. Bring the patties to room temperature 20 minutes before grilling.

Oil the grill, place it 4 inches (10 cm) above the heat source, and sear the burgers 5-6 minutes per side. Cook the burgers until they are a rich, crusty golden brown on the outside, and just pink on the inside. Serve at once with Fresh Mint Chutney.

FRESH MINT CHUTNEY

Serve cool or at room temperature with the grilled lamb burgers.

1	clove garlic, chopped	1
1/2 tsp.	salt	2 mL
2 cups	fresh mint, lightly packed	500 mL
	(about 4 small bunches)	
1/2 cup	chopped onion	125 mL
1/4 cup	toasted pine nuts	50 mL
1/4 tsp.	*each* ground cumin and black pepper	1 mL
1/2 cup	olive oil	125 mL
3 tbsp.	fresh lemon juice	45 mL

In a food processor fitted with a steel blade, process the garlic and salt to a paste. Add the mint and process until very finely minced, scraping down the sides. Add the onion and pine nuts, and process to a fine mince. Add the cumin and pepper. With the motor running, add the olive oil in a thin, steady stream. Finally, add the lemon juice. The finished sauce should be like a chunky vinaigrette.

Transfer the sauce to a glass container, and allow to rest in a cool place several hours before using. Do not serve this chutney sauce cold, as it will firm up. Serve at room temperature so that the sauce may be drizzled over the burgers.

TENDERLOIN KEBABS

Pork tenderloin is a treat any time of the year. In summer, grilled to quick perfection with fresh vegetables, it is incomparable. Serves 6.

1 - 1 1/2 lbs.	pork tenderloin	500-750 g
2	eggs	2
1 tsp.	water	5 mL
1 cup	fine dry bread crumbs	250 mL
2 tbsp.	grated Parmesan cheese	30 mL
1 tbsp.	chopped fresh herbs: parsley, oregano and thyme	15 mL
1/2 tsp.	freshly ground black pepper	2 mL
1/2 cup	all-purpose flour	125 mL
6	*each* onion quarters, cherry tomatoes, bell pepper quarters, Japanese eggplant slices	6
	Kebab Sauce (recipe follows)	

Slice the meat diagonally into 1/2 inch (1 cm) pieces. Pound to 1/4 inch (5 mm) thickness. Beat together the eggs and water. In another bowl, mix the bread crumbs, cheese, herbs and pepper. Dredge the pork slices in the flour, dip in the egg mixture, then coat with the crumb mixture. About 20 minutes before cooking time, soak 18 6 inch (15 cm) wooden skewers in water. Weave the meat onto the skewers alternately with the vegetables.

Heat the barbecue to hot. Grill the kebabs 10 minutes, turning and brushing with Kebab Sauce frequently. Reduce the heat to medium and cook 5 minutes longer or until the meat is golden and the vegetables are heated through. Place the kebabs on a serving platter and spoon on extra Kebab Sauce.

KEBAB SAUCE

1 cup	pineapple juice	250 mL
4 tbsp.	oil	60 mL
2 tbsp.	brown sugar	30 mL
1	clove garlic, crushed	1
1/2 tsp.	curry powder	2 mL

Bring all ingredients to a boil in a saucepan and boil until reduced by one quarter. Keep warm.

HINESE-STYLE FINGER RIBS

This recipe makes restaurant-style appetizer "finger" ribs, only better! Serve them as an appetizer, with big goblets of iced tea. Or serve them as a main course, with a stir-fry of colourful snow peas and assorted bell peppers and steamed white rice. Makes appetizers for 6.

3	whole slabs pork baby back ribs, cut in half to make 6 portions	3
6 quarts	boiling water	6 L
1 cup + 1 tbsp.	cider vinegar	265 mL
1 tbsp.	*each* salt, pepper and Chinese 5-spice, combined	15 mL
1	10 oz. (284 mL) bottle Chinese-style sweet'n'sour sauce	1
2 tbsp.	*each* soy sauce and dry sherry	30 mL
1 tbsp.	brown sugar	15 mL
10 drops	bottled hot pepper sauce	10 drops

Heat the barbecue to medium-hot.

Place the rib portions in a colander, and pour boiling water over them to scald. The meat will turn opaque. Pat the ribs completely dry. Lightly oil the grill, place the ribs on it 6-8 inches (15-20 cm) above the heat source, and brush the meat with 1 cup (250 mL) of the cider vinegar. Slowly cook the ribs, brushing with vinegar and turning as they brown. After the initial searing, sprinkle the 5-spice mixture lightly on both sides. Cook the ribs slowly, about 12-15 minutes per side. Meanwhile, combine the sweet'n'sour sauce, soy sauce, sherry, brown sugar, hot pepper sauce and the remaining 1 tbsp. (15 mL) vinegar in a small saucepan. Simmer 5-7 minutes until bubbly. Set aside.

Grill the ribs 10-15 more minutes per side, basting frequently with the sauce, until the ribs are highly glazed, the meat pulls away slightly from the tips of the bones, and the ribs are tender. The edges should be slightly charred.

Let the meat rest 8 minutes, then carve straight down between ribs to make serving sections of 1-3 ribs. Serve any remaining sauce separately, for dipping.

PRAIRIE-STYLE COFFEE-GLAZED RIBS

These ribs are a cowboy's delight, grilled to a glazed turn with a coffee-punched barbecue sauce. Ladle up a side of smokey beans, pass a bowl of crisp cabbage cole slaw, and don't forget the hot buttermilk biscuits! Serves 4.

4	whole slabs pork baby back ribs	4
2 cups	freshly brewed strong black coffee, at room temperature	500 mL
1/3 cup	cider vinegar	75 mL
	salt and pepper to taste	

Barbecue Sauce:

1	12 oz. (365 mL) bottle chili sauce	1
3/4 cup	ketchup	175 mL
8 tbsp.	butter	120 mL
3/4 cup	freshly brewed strong black coffee	175 mL
2 tbsp.	instant coffee crystals (optional — for a stronger coffee taste)	30 mL
4 tbsp.	Worcestershire sauce	60 mL
1/3 cup	molasses	75 mL
1 tbsp.	chili powder	15 mL
1/2 tsp.	*each* cinnamon and allspice	2 mL
	salt and pepper to taste	

Prepare the barbecue sauce several hours ahead of time. In a large saucepan combine the chili sauce, ketchup, butter, the 3/4 cup (175 mL) coffee, coffee crystals, Worcestershire sauce, molasses, chili powder, cinnamon and allspice. Simmer the sauce, partially covered, over medium-low heat for 45 minutes until glossy and thickened. Stir occasionally to prevent scorching. Season to taste with salt and pepper. Set aside until ready to barbecue.

Combine the 2 cups (500 mL) coffee and the vinegar. Brush over the meat on both sides, and allow the ribs to sit at room temperature 45 minutes.

Heat the barbecue to medium-hot and lightly oil the grill. Place the ribs meaty side down, 4 inches (10 cm) from the heat source, and sear 7 minutes on each side. Season lightly with salt and pepper. Brush the ribs with the coffee vinegar mixture, and cook 7 minutes per side. Grill the ribs about 12-15 more minutes per side, turning the slabs several times and basting with barbecue sauce. The finished ribs should be sticky, highly glazed, nicely charred at the edges, and just tender. Let the ribs rest 10 minutes. Serve with thin, sharp knives for cutting down between the ribs, and put any remaining sauce into bowls for dipping.

ARINATED BARBECUE PORK LOIN

Tender, tasty pork loin, marinated with herbs and grilled slowly, is a mouth-watering hit on a summer evening. Let it turn on the barbecue spit if you have one, or turn the meat often on an oiled grill. A helpful hint: the sauce tends to flare on the hot barbecue, so make a drip catcher out of foil. A crisp salad from the deli department and Grilled Stuffed Potatoes (p. 78) are wonderful accompaniments. Serves 6-8.

2 lbs.	rolled boneless loin of pork	1 kg
1 cup	prepared barbecue sauce	250 mL
1	clove garlic, crushed	1
4 tbsp.	cider vinegar	60 mL
2 tbsp.	liquid honey	30 mL
1 tbsp.	soy or teriyaki sauce	15 mL
1/2 tsp.	*each* dried oregano, thyme, ginger, salt and pepper	2 mL

Place the pork in a zip-lock or other sealable plastic bag. Combine and pour in the remaining ingredients. Refrigerate, turning often, for about 2 hours or up to 1 day.

Heat the barbecue to medium-low and place the marinated meat on an oiled rack. Cover with a lid or foil tent and roast, turning and basting with marinade every 15 minutes, until a meat thermometer reads 160°F (70°C) and the meat is crusty and dark brown on the outside, and white and moist inside.

BERRY PATCH GLAZED PORK RIBS

These vibrantly glazed berry-flavoured pork ribs are utterly delectable, and so simple to prepare for summer guests! Mound the ribs on a festive platter and scatter fresh berries over the finished dish for a gorgeous, mouth-watering presentation. Serve with a crisp green field lettuce salad, grilled corn-on-the-cob slathered in butter and hot garlic bread. Serves 6.

	Berry Patch Barbecue Glaze (recipe follows)	
6	whole slabs pork baby back ribs	6
2	oranges, cut in half	2
	salt and pepper to taste	
1/2 cup	raspberry-flavoured vinegar	125 mL
	fresh raspberries and/or strawberries for garnish	
	fresh berry leaves for garnish	

Prepare the barbecue glaze several hours before using to allow the flavours to blend.

Bring the pork ribs to room temperature, rubbing both sides with cut oranges. Allow to sit 45 minutes while preparing the barbecue.

Heat the barbecue to medium-hot. Lightly oil the grill and place it 6 inches (15 cm) from the heat source. Sear the ribs, meaty side down, for 6 minutes. Season with salt and pepper, and turn the ribs. Sear the other side 4-5 minutes. Continue to grill the ribs, brushing generously with the raspberry vinegar, about 12 minutes per side.

Begin basting the ribs with Berry Patch Barbecue Glaze, turning every few minutes, for a total additional cooking time of 15-20 minutes. The finished ribs should be tender, the meat should pull away from the bone tips slightly, and the meat should be highly glazed and slightly charred.

Remove the ribs to a platter, and allow to rest 8 minutes before serving. To garnish, scatter fresh berries around the platter, and tuck in fresh berry leaves. Serve with small, thin sharp knives for cutting down between each rib. Serve any remaining sauce in a small bowl for dipping.

BERRY PATCH BARBECUE GLAZE

This wonderful glaze is also delicious with barbecued hens, game, chicken, duck and tiger prawns. The sauce may be prepared up to one week ahead, and stored tightly capped and chilled. Bring it to room temperature before using.

2 tbsp.	*each* butter and vegetable oil	30 mL
1/2 cup	finely minced shallots	125 mL
2	small cloves garlic, minced	2
12 oz.	raspberry preserves	365 mL
4 tbsp.	raspberry-flavoured vinegar	60 mL
2 tbsp.	Worcestershire sauce	30 mL
3 tbsp.	dry sherry	45 mL
1 tsp.	dried thyme	5 mL
pinch	ground cloves	pinch
12 drops	bottled hot pepper sauce	12 drops
3 tbsp.	butter	45 mL
	salt and pepper to taste	

Heat the butter and oil in a saucepan over medium-high heat until bubbly. Add the minced shallots and garlic, and sauté, stirring, until translucent and pale golden in colour. Add the raspberry preserves, vinegar, Worcestershire sauce, sherry, thyme, cloves and hot pepper sauce. Bring the mixture to a simmer, reduce to low heat and cook 45 minutes, stirring frequently. Finally, whisk in the butter until the sauce is melted and bubbly. Season with salt and pepper to taste. Remove from heat, and set aside to cool before using.

The Easy Gourmet features a photograph of this recipe on page 35.

I TALIAN SAUSAGE AND PEPPER SANDWICH

Nothing entices hungry patrons of New York's famed San Gennaro Festival more than the delectable aromas that waft from the stands offering grilled sausage and pepper sandwiches. Try this recipe for your next party get-together. Serves 6-8.

12	fresh Italian sausages, a combination of	12
	sweet and hot, about 2 lbs. (1 kg)	
1 1/3 cups	olive oil	325 mL
4 tbsp.	red wine vinegar	60 mL
2 tsp.	*each* dried oregano and basil	10 mL
2 tsp.	sugar	10 mL
8-10 drops	bottled hot pepper sauce	8-10 drops
3	*each* red, yellow and green	3
	bell peppers, quartered	
2-3	long loaves Italian or French bread (baguettes)	2-3
	Capered Mustard Butter (recipe follows)	

Prick the sausages in several places, cover with water and simmer 5-6 minutes until the sausages turn opaque and are slightly firm. Cool in water, and remove. Pat the sausages dry. Slice each sausage open, leaving halves attached in the middle. Heat the barbecue to medium-hot.

Combine the olive oil, vinegar, oregano, basil, sugar and hot pepper sauce. Lightly oil the grill, add the sausages and peppers, and baste with the oil mixture. Grill 4-6 inches (10-15 cm) above the heat source, until the sausages and peppers are rich golden brown on all sides, and the peppers are very tender, about 14-18 minutes.

Meanwhile, cut each bread into 3 sections. Split each section open, leaving two halves attached. Open the breads up flat. Brush the cut sides lightly with the oil mixture.

Remove the sausages and peppers to a warm platter. Place the oiled breads on the grill, and toast 2-3 minutes until golden brown. Remove from grill. Slather each bun with softened, prepared Capered Mustard Butter, tuck in the sausages and an assortment of peppers, and serve at once piping hot.

CAPERED MUSTARD BUTTER

1/2 lb.	softened butter	250 g
2	cloves garlic, minced	2
3 tbsp.	capers, drained	45 mL
3 tbsp.	pimiento, drained	45 mL
1/3 cup	minced fresh parsley	75 mL
2 tbsp.	*each* honey mustard and cider vinegar	30 mL
	salt and freshly ground black pepper to taste	
1/4 tsp.	paprika	1 mL

In a food processor, beat the softened butter, garlic, capers, pimiento, parsley, mustard and vinegar until fluffy and well blended. Season to taste with salt, pepper and paprika. Refrigerate, and soften before serving.

GINGER-TERIYAKI VEGETABLE KEBABS

Brush vegetables with this subtle tangy-sweet sauce and grill them alongside the entrée, and you've got a vitamin-packed side dish that tastes like summer. Choose vegetables that will finish cooking together: cherry tomatoes, tiny pearl onions, wedges of sweet bell pepper, zucchini, mushrooms and chunks of eggplant. Makes 1 cup (250 mL).

1/2 cup	oil	125 mL
3 tbsp.	teriyaki sauce	45 mL
4 tbsp.	red wine vinegar	60 mL
1 tsp.	finely chopped fresh ginger	5 mL
1	clove garlic, minced	1
	a few grinds of black pepper	

Combine all ingredients thoroughly. Brush the sauce on skewers of vegetables. Turning and basting frequently, grill 4-6 minutes, or until tender, on medium heat.

SWEET-AND-SOUR FRUIT KEBABS

Grilled kebabs of fresh summer fruit can replace vegetables for a delightful surprise at a summer dinner party. Choose firm fruits that will hold their shape on the barbecue, and remember fresh peeled, cored pineapple is available all year round in the produce department. Serve it all up with sweet-and-sour Fruit Kebab Sauce, a crispy green salad, robust multi-grain bread and ice cream for dessert. Makes 5-6 kebabs.

1	fresh pineapple	1
1	large red apple	1
2	medium navel oranges	2
1	nectarine	1
2	apricots	2
1	banana	1
	Fruit Kebab Sauce (recipe follows)	

Cut the fruit into 1-2 inch (2.5-5 cm) chunks and thread alternately on skewers. Grill, brushing often with Fruit Kebab Sauce, until the fruit is tender and juicy. Serve at once.

FRUIT KEBAB SAUCE

Makes 1 cup (250 mL).

1/2 cup	liquid honey	125 mL
1/2 cup	vinegar	125 mL
2 tbsp.	vegetable oil	30 mL
1	clove garlic, crushed	1
1/2 tsp.	curry, or to taste	2 mL

Combine all ingredients thoroughly.

Opposite: (Top to bottom) Hickory-Smoked Chicken Quarters (page 42) and Berry Patch Glazed Pork Ribs (page 30).

HERB-GRILLED VEGETABLES

Fresh vegetables take on a distinctive, delicious flavour done on the barbecue. Brushed with this special herb butter, they are irresistible! You'll want to try other vegetables: parboiled whole carrots, whole onions, beets, potatoes — almost anything goes. Serves 4.

3/4 cup	melted butter	175 mL
2 tbsp.	fresh lemon juice	30 mL
2 tbsp.	chopped fresh herbs such as parsley, thyme, oregano, rosemary	30 mL
4	zucchini or crookneck squash, split lengthwise	4
4	ears corn-on-the-cob	4
2	*each* red and yellow bell peppers, quartered lengthwise	2
12	whole mushroom caps	12

Combine the butter, lemon juice and herbs. Brush the mixture over the vegetables and grill, turning and basting frequently.

The Easy Gourmet features a photograph of this recipe on the front cover.

FAVOURITE GRILLED CORN-ON-THE-COB

Barbecued corn-on-the-cob is the taste of summer! Serve it with any grilled entrée. Serves 4.

4	ears corn-on-the-cob	4
4 tbsp.	softened butter	60 mL
	seasoning salt, herbs to taste	

Husk the corn, leaving the tender inner leaves attached. Pull the leaves back gently and remove the silk. Rub each ear of corn with 1 tbsp. (15 mL) butter. Sprinkle lightly with seasoning salt or herbs. Press the leaves back over the ears. Soak in water for 20 minutes. Drain, and place on an oiled grill. Cook 12-15 minutes, turning several times. Remove from grill, discard the husks and serve.

BARBECUED PORK CHOPS WITH CORNICHON BUTTER

The next time you fire up the grill, try these tantalizing barbecued pork chops — slightly charred on the outside, juicy and succulent on the inside, with the heady flavour of tarragon and sherry vinegar in the simple marinade. Top each chop with a knob of chilled Cornichon Butter and accompany with grilled new potatoes and fresh steamed green beans. Serves 4.

6 tbsp.	olive oil	90 mL
1	large clove garlic, crushed	1
2 tbsp.	fresh lemon juice	30 mL
2 tbsp.	sherry vinegar	30 mL
2 tbsp.	*each* finely minced fresh tarragon and parsley	30 mL
4	pork loin or rib chops, each 1 1/4 inches (3 cm) thick	4
	salt and coarsely ground pepper to taste	
	Cornichon Butter (recipe follows)	
	fresh tarragon sprigs for garnish	

Combine the olive oil, garlic, lemon juice, vinegar, tarragon and parsley, whisking to combine. Brush marinade over the chops and allow to stand at room temperature 25 minutes.

Heat the barbecue to medium-hot. Lightly oil the grill and cook the chops 4-6 inches (10-15 cm) above the heat source, turning only once or twice, until golden brown and slightly charred on the outside, juicy and just no longer pink on the inside, about 15-18 minutes total cooking time. Season the chops with salt and pepper after searing both sides. The finished chops should feel just firm when pressed with your finger, but not hard. Remove the chops from the grill, and allow to stand 5 minutes before serving for the juices to absorb. Top each chop with a generous knob of chilled Cornichon Butter, garnish with a sprig of tarragon and serve.

CORNICHON BUTTER

Prepare this savoury butter 1-3 days before serving, for maximum flavour. Cornichons are tiny sour pickled gherkins, the finest imported from France. Use any leftover butter to top grilled chicken or fish.

1/2 lb.	softened butter	250 g
1/3 cup	French-style sour cornichon pickles, drained and very finely chopped	75 mL
3 tbsp.	sherry vinegar	45 mL
3 tbsp.	*each* minced fresh tarragon and parsley	45 mL
	salt and coarsely ground black pepper to taste	

In a food processor, cream together the butter, pickles, vinegar, tarragon and parsley. Beat until fluffy and well blended. Season to taste with salt and generous grindings of pepper. Store the prepared butter in a tightly sealed crock, or shape it into a log and wrap tightly in waxed paper. Chill up to 3 days before using.

PORK AND APRICOT KEBABS

Two ways to make barbecued kebabs as tender and moist as they can be are to marinate them, and to serve them with a creamy sauce. In this recipe, the kebabs are treated to both — a zesty citrus marinade and a sauce that is so simple, quick and delicious, you have to taste it to believe it! Complete the meal with saffron coloured rice and a green salad. Serves 4.

Orange Marinade:

3 tbsp.	freshly squeezed orange juice	45 mL
1 tsp.	grated orange rind	5 mL
2 tbsp.	oil	30 mL
1	small onion, minced	1
1/2 tsp.	paprika	2 mL
1/4 tsp.	*each* salt and pepper	1 mL

Kebabs:

1 lb.	pork loin chops, tenderloin end, trimmed, cut in 20 cubes, *each* about 1 1/2 inches (4 cm)	500 g
4	wooden skewers, 12 inches (30 cm) long, soaked in water for 20 minutes	4
4	slices bacon, halved and rolled	4
8	bay leaves	8
4	apricots, halved, fresh or canned (drained)	4
	apricots for garnish	

Fruity Sauce:

1/2 cup	sour cream	125 mL
3 tbsp.	apricot jam	45 mL

To make the marinade, combine the orange juice, rind, oil, onion, paprika, salt and pepper in a shallow dish. Toss the pork in the marinade, cover and refrigerate for 2 hours, turning occasionally.

Remove the pork from the marinade, reserving the marinade, and thread 5 pieces of pork onto each skewer, alternating with other ingredients in this order: pork, bacon roll, pork, bay leaf, apricot half, pork, apricot half, bacon roll, bay leaf and 2 pieces pork.

Heat the barbecue to hot. Cook the kebabs for 10 minutes, then reduce the heat to medium low and cook a further 5-10 minutes. Turn the kebabs and brush occasionally with the marinade throughout the cooking time. Place the kebabs on a serving platter and garnish with apricots.

To make the sauce, beat together the sour cream and jam and spoon it into a serving dish. Serve the kebabs hot with the sauce on the side.

UPER SIMPLE GRILLED CHICKEN

Sometimes the simplest pleasures are the best. This recipe proves it — only two ingredients, and no-fail results on the barbecue! Try bottled vinaigrette, ranch-style or Russian dressing, or your favourite salad dressing. Grilled Vegetable Salad (p. 80) sets it off perfectly. Serves 4.

2	small whole chickens, each 2-3 lbs. (1-1.5 kg)	2
1 cup	bottled salad dressing	250 mL

Cut down either side of the backbone of each chicken and discard bones. Spread the body apart, skin side up, and press flat.

Heat the barbecue to medium. Oil the grill and cook the chicken 10 minutes, basting frequently with dressing. Turn, reduce heat if necessary to prevent fires, and cook 10-15 more minutes or until done, brushing often with dressing. Serve warm.

HICKORY-SMOKED CHICKEN QUARTERS

When summer is upon us and the barbecue is fired up, no get-together seems complete without at least one "finger-licking good" recipe. This is it —a grilled chicken dish that is wildly popular with kids and adults alike. The sauce has a tantalizing smokey flavour, accented with citrus marmalade, molasses and cider vinegar, guaranteed to keep them coming back for more! Round out the feast with Favourite Grilled Corn-on-the-Cob (p. 37), a pot of molasses-baked beans, crisp cole slaw (your own or from the deli department), big sweet gherkins, and a basket of hot buttermilk biscuits. Serves 8.

	Smokey Barbecue Sauce (recipe follows)	
4 tbsp.	*each* corn oil and melted butter	60 mL
2/3 cup	cider vinegar	150 mL
2 tsp.	liquid smoke	10 mL
2	3 - 3 1/2 lb. (1.5 - 1.75 kg)	2
	whole frying chickens, quartered	
	salt and pepper to taste	

Prepare the Smokey Barbecue Sauce up to 3 days in advance, stored chilled and tightly capped. Bring it to room temperature before using.

Combine the corn oil, melted butter, vinegar and liquid smoke. Brush over the chicken quarters, and allow to marinate at room temperature while preparing the barbecue. Heat the barbecue to medium-hot. Oil the grill, place it 6 inches (15 cm) above the heat source and cook the chicken 10 minutes per side, turning once. Season with salt and pepper after searing. Begin brushing the chicken with the Smokey Barbecue Sauce after the first 20 minutes, continuing to grill slowly until the meat is tender and the skin is a rich brown with slightly charred edges. Total cooking time will be about 45 minutes, less for the breast pieces. Do not overcook. Transfer the grilled chicken to a platter, and allow to sit 10 minutes before serving to allow the juices to re-absorb. Serve any remaining sauce in a dipping bowl.

SMOKEY BARBECUE SAUCE

4 tbsp.	*each* butter and corn oil	60 mL
1	medium onion, minced	1
1	9 oz. (250 mL) jar bitter orange marmalade	1
1	16 oz. (455 mL) bottle smokey-flavoured barbecue sauce	1
2 tbsp.	*each* Worcestershire sauce, molasses and cider vinegar	30 mL
1 cup	beer or non-alcoholic beer	250 mL
1 tsp.	liquid smoke	5 mL
1/2 tsp.	ground cloves	2 mL

Heat the butter and oil in a deep saucepan until bubbly. Add the onion and sauté until softened and pale golden. Add the marmalade, barbecue sauce, Worcestershire sauce, molasses, vinegar, beer, liquid smoke and cloves. Bring the mixture to a simmer, stirring to incorporate all ingredients and melt the marmalade completely. Reduce the heat to low, partially cover the sauce, and cook until thickened and glossy and the flavours are blended, about 50 minutes, stirring occasionally. Adjust seasoning to taste.

Remove the sauce from the heat and allow to cool to room temperature. Store in glass jars, tightly capped and chilled, until ready to use. Bring the sauce to room temperature before using.

The Easy Gourmet features a photograph of this recipe on page 35.

TERIYAKI CHICKEN ROLLS

This special dish is ideal for entertaining with its savoury stuffing, tangy teriyaki glaze, and a presentation that looks like you worked on it all day. Steamed rice and grilled fresh zucchini complete this memorable barbecue. Serves 8.

4	boneless whole chicken breasts, about 2 lbs. (1 kg)	4

Oriental Stuffing:

1/3 cup	brown rice	75 mL
3	slices bacon, very finely chopped	3
1/3 cup	finely chopped mushrooms	75 mL
1/3 cup	finely chopped water chestnuts	75 mL
2 tbsp.	chopped fresh parsley	30 mL
1 1/2 tsp.	soy sauce	7 mL

Teriyaki Glaze:

2/3 cup	honey	150 mL
1/2 cup	soy sauce	125 mL
4 tsp.	grated fresh ginger	20 mL
3	cloves garlic, crushed	3
2 tbsp.	oil	30 mL
	chopped parsley for garnish	

Cut the chicken breasts in half. Place each piece skin side down between 2 sheets of waxed paper and beat with a meat mallet or rolling pin until it is half the original thickness. Cover and refrigerate until ready to stuff.

To make the stuffing, cook the rice according to package directions. Let cool. In a small saucepan, fry the bacon until crisp. Add the mushrooms and cook for 1 minute. Remove the bacon and mushrooms with a slotted spoon and stir into the rice with the water chestnuts, parsley and soy sauce. Set aside.

To make the glaze, combine the honey, soy sauce, ginger, garlic and oil in a small bowl, stirring to mix well.

Lay the chicken skin side down. Place about 2 tbsp. (30 mL) of stuffing in the centre of each piece. Wrap them up neatly like parcels, folding ends and sides over the stuffing to enclose. Secure each parcel with wooden toothpicks.

Heat the barbecue to medium-hot. Grill the rolls 20-25 minutes, turning occasionally, until almost cooked, lowering the heat if necessary. Cook for 5 more minutes, turning and brushing frequently with the glaze.

Remove the toothpicks and arrange the chicken on a serving platter. Heat the remaining glaze. Pour a little of the glaze over the chicken and serve the rest on the side. Garnish with chopped parsley.

CHICKEN AND PEPPER BROCHETTES

Chicken tenders, the tenderloin pieces of chicken found in the poultry section, make succulent kebabs for barbecuing. Serve this dish with simple grilled potatoes and a bright green salad. Makes 6 brochettes.

1 cup	vegetable oil	250 mL
4 tbsp.	fresh lemon juice	60 mL
4 tbsp.	white wine vinegar	60 mL
2	cloves garlic, crushed	2
2 tsp.	seasoned salt	10 mL
1/2 tsp.	dry mustard	2 mL
1/2 tsp.	salt	2 mL
1/4 tsp.	dry red chiles, crushed (optional)	1 mL
1 lb.	chicken tenders, about 20 whole tenders	500 g
1	*each* red and yellow bell pepper	1

Combine the oil, lemon juice, vinegar, garlic, seasoned salt, mustard, salt and chiles in a jar and shake well. Place the tenders and marinade in a zip-lock bag. Seal and refrigerate for 1 hour or overnight. Heat the barbecue to medium-hot. Cut the peppers into 1 inch (2.5 cm) chunks. Soak six 10 inch (25 cm) wooden skewers in water for 20 minutes. Weave the marinated chicken tenders on the skewers alternately with the peppers.

Cook 5-6 minutes, turning once and brushing with marinade, and serve hot.

C ITRUS GLAZED TURKEY KEBABS

These grilled kebabs are gorgeous to look at, even better to eat! Using economical, no-waste, low-fat, boneless turkey is a bonus, and the meat department boasts fresh turkey in a wonderful array of cuts all year round. Serve with dipping sauce, hot steamed rice and grilled fresh summer squashes. Serves 6-8.

3 lbs.	boned turkey pieces (combination breast and thigh meat)	1.5 kg
1/2 cup	olive or vegetable oil	125 mL
1/4 cup	*each* fresh orange juice, lemon juice and dry sherry	50 mL
1 1/2 tsp.	dried thyme	7 mL
1 tsp.	paprika	5 mL
2 tsp.	*each* grated lemon and orange rind	10 mL
1	fresh pineapple, stemmed, peeled and cut into 1 1/2 inch (3.5 cm) chunks	1
2	large onions, peeled and cut into 1 1/2 inch (3.5 cm) chunks, separated into layers	2
	salt and pepper to taste	
	Citrus Dipping Sauce (recipe follows)	

Cut the turkey into 1 1/2 inch (3.5 cm) cubes.(Partially freeze it, if desired, to firm slightly for ease in cubing.) Whisk together the oil, orange and lemon juices, sherry, thyme, paprika, lemon and orange rinds until emulsified. Toss the marinade with the cubed turkey meat, and set aside 1-2 hours. Meanwhile, cube the pineapple and onions. Blanch the onion slices in simmering water 1-2 minutes, and drain thoroughly. If you are using wooden skewers, soak them in warm water 20 minutes to prevent burning while grilling.

Heat the barbecue to medium-hot. While the coals are heating, prepare the skewers by removing the turkey from the marinade and threading alternately with pineapple cubes and several slices of onion, beginning and ending each skewer with turkey.

Lightly oil the grill and cook the kebabs 4-6 inches (10-15 cm) above the heat source, turning every 5-6 minutes and brushing with any remaining marinade. Season with salt and pepper during the final minutes of cooking time. Cook until the turkey is tender and a rich golden brown with slightly charred edges, about 13-15 minutes total. Remove the skewers, arrange them on a large platter lined with green leaves and serve with Citrus Dipping Sauce.

CITRUS DIPPING SAUCE

1/4 lb.	butter	125 g
1	onion, minced	1
1 tbsp.	brown sugar	15 mL
1	whole lemon, seeded and ground, including rind	1
1/2 cup	lemon marmalade	125 mL
2 tbsp.	*each* prepared horseradish and dry sherry	30 mL
1/2 cup	fresh orange juice	125 mL
1 tbsp.	finely grated orange rind	15 mL
	salt and pepper to taste	

Heat the butter until bubbly over medium-high heat, and add the onion. Sauté, stirring, until softened and pale golden. Add the brown sugar, ground lemon, marmalade, horseradish, sherry, orange juice and orange rind. Bring the mixture to a simmer, and cook over low heat 25 minutes until glossy, thickened and the consistency of preserves. Season with salt and pepper to taste, and set aside to cool to room temperature. Serve the sauce cool or barely warm with the grilled turkey skewers.

Note: This sauce also makes an excellent basting barbecue sauce for duck, all kinds of poultry, pork, lamb or shellfish. Baste during the final 10 minutes of grilling only, to prevent burning.

GRILLED TURKEY BURGERS WITH GARDEN CHUTNEY

Ground turkey is a wonderful buy — nutritious, low in fat, and versatile. These burgers prove the point! Combine the meat mixture the night before to allow the flavours to blend, prepare the chutney ahead of time, and when friends or family pour in, just fire up the coals for an instant winner! Serve with a red potato salad, warm garlic bread and Vegetable Medley with Creamy Herb Dip (p. 87). Serves 4-6.

6	slices bacon, finely minced	6
	(about 4 oz. (125 g))	
1 cup	minced onion	250 mL
2 tbsp.	butter	30 mL
2	cloves garlic, minced	2
1/3 cup	*each* currants and chopped walnuts	75 mL
1 1/2 lbs.	ground turkey	750 g
1/3 cup	minced fresh parsley	75 mL
1 tsp.	*each* salt, dried thyme, marjoram and sage, crumbled	5 mL
1	egg, lightly beaten	1
1/4 cup	*each* grated Parmesan cheese and fresh bread crumbs	50 mL
1/2 tsp.	black pepper	2 mL
	Garden Chutney (recipe follows)	

Sauté the minced bacon in a skillet over medium-high heat until transluscent. Add the onion, butter and garlic, and continue to sauté until the mixture is tender and pale golden in colour. Add the currants and walnuts, and heat 1-2 minutes to plump the currants. Set the mixture aside to cool to room temperature.

Combine the ground turkey with the cooled onion mixture, adding the parsley, salt, thyme, marjoram, sage, egg, Parmesan, bread crumbs and pepper. Combine gently but thoroughly, kneading several minutes to bind the ingredients. Cover the mixture with plastic wrap, and chill several hours or overnight.

Bring the turkey mixture to room temperature 45 minutes while heating the barbecue to hot. Shape the turkey meat into 4-6 oval patties, each about 3/4 inch (1.5 cm) thick, with moistened hands. Lightly oil the grill, and grill the burgers 6-8 minutes per side, 4-6 inches (10-15 cm) above the heat source, turning once or twice with a wide metal spatula. The finished burgers should be crusty and slightly charred on the outside, cooked through but still juicy on the inside (the juice should run clear, with no trace of pink, when the burger is pierced with the tip of a sharp knife). Remove the burgers from the grill, and serve piping hot, each topped with a generous spoonful or two of Garden Chutney.

GARDEN CHUTNEY

2 tbsp.	butter	30 mL
3 tbsp.	olive or vegetable oil	45 mL
1	large onion, chopped	1
2	tart green apples, peeled and chopped	2
4	green tomatoes, chopped	4
1 tsp.	*each* whole mustard seed, celery seed and salt	5 mL
1/3 cup	*each* light brown sugar and cider vinegar	75 mL
1/4 tsp.	ground cloves	1 mL
1	2 inch (5 cm) whole cinnamon stick	1
pinch	cayenne pepper	pinch
10 drops	bottled hot pepper sauce	10 drops

In a large saucepan, heat the butter and oil over medium-high heat. Add the onion and apples, and sauté until just softened. Add the tomatoes, and sauté until the juices are released and reabsorbed. The vegetables and fruit should be pulpy, softened, and slightly glossy.

Add the mustard seed, celery seed, salt, sugar, vinegar, cloves, cinnamon stick and cayenne pepper. Stir to combine, bring the mixture to a simmer, reduce heat to low and cook, partially covered, for 45 minutes, stirring frequently. Season with hot pepper sauce, taste and correct for seasonings. Cool to room temperature. Store the chutney in tightly capped glass jars, refrigerated. Serve cool or at room temperature with the hot burgers.

MAHOGANY MAPLE-GLAZED GAME HENS

These delectable glazed hens are pure Canadian — brushed with a maple syrup barbecue sauce and grilled to a rich, crispy, golden brown finish. Serve these hens hot off the grill with wild rice tossed with toasted pecans, fresh asparagus, a leafy green salad, and warm dinner rolls. Serves 4.

	Maple Syrup Glaze (recipe follows)	
4	fresh Rock Cornish game hens,	4
	1 lb. (500 g) each	
2	lemons	2
4 tsp.	dried thyme	20 mL
	nutmeg to taste	
4 tbsp.	*each* melted butter and oil	60 mL
	salt and pepper to taste	
	lemon slices, fresh sprigs thyme and	
	maple leaves for garnish	

Prepare the glaze 1-2 hours ahead of time to allow the flavours to blend. Set aside at room temperature.

Rinse the hens with cold water and pat completely dry. Split each hen open and "butterfly" by cutting along the backbone. Pull the hens open, place on a flat work surface, and press flat with your hand, cracking the backbone if necessary. Bend the wings and tuck under to hold hens flat.

Rub the hens with cut lemons on both sides. Sprinkle with thyme and season lightly on both sides with nutmeg. Allow the hens to stand at room temperature while preparing the barbecue.

Heat the barbecue to medium-hot. Lightly oil the grill, and place the hens on it, skin side down. Brush the hens with the butter-oil mixture, and season with salt and pepper. Cook the hens 6 inches (15 cm) above the heat source, about 5 minutes per side, turning once. Brush with glaze, and continue to grill, turning and basting on both sides until highly glazed, shiny, and a deep, rich golden brown, about 10 minutes more per side. The finished hens should just feel firm when pressed with your finger, and the legs should move freely in the joints.

Remove the hens to warmed plates, and allow to rest 5-7 minutes before serving to allow the juices to absorb. Garnish with lemon slices, fresh sprigs of thyme and single maple leaves. Serve any remaining sauce separately to spoon over each portion.

MAPLE SYRUP GLAZE

Use this glaze for the delectable hens, or for basting ham, duck, chicken, pork, ribs or sausages.

4 tbsp.	butter	60 mL
1/3 cup	minced shallots or onion	75 mL
1 1/2 cups	pure maple syrup	375 mL
	(medium or dark grade)	
2 tbsp.	*each* fresh lemon juice	30 mL
	and cider vinegar	
3 tbsp.	brown sugar, firmly packed	45 mL
2 tsp.	finely grated lemon rind	10 mL
4 tbsp.	butter, chilled and cut into pieces	60 mL
	salt to taste	

Heat the butter in a saucepan over medium-high heat until bubbly. Add the minced shallots and sauté until softened and pale golden. Add the maple syrup, lemon juice, cider vinegar, brown sugar and lemon rind. Simmer over medium-low heat, stirring frequently, 20 minutes until bubbly, thickened and syrupy. Reduce the heat to low, and whisk in the butter, piece by piece, adding each piece when the previous one has melted. Add a pinch of salt to taste, whisk the sauce smooth, and remove from heat. Set sauce aside until ready to use.

NEW WAVE BUFFALO CHICKEN WINGS

The traditional (and wildly popular!) Buffalo Chicken Wings are done up in a big black iron skillet, with a heady, spicy sauce. Pubs made them popular, but served anywhere they are addictively delicious and just plain fun to eat! This version is served up with the traditional bowl of blue cheese dressing for dipping, and icy cold celery for munching (we've added other vegetables as well). Makes 24 wings.

24	chicken wings (the entire wing)	24
4 tbsp.	corn oil	60 mL
3 tbsp.	bottled hot pepper sauce	45 mL
3 tbsp.	*each* cider vinegar and fresh lemon juice	45 mL
1 cup	beer or non-alcoholic beer	250 mL
6 tbsp.	hot melted butter	90 mL
1/4 - 1/2 tsp.	cayenne pepper (to taste)	1-2 mL
1 1/2 cups	chilled blue cheese dressing (restaurant style, found bottled in the produce department)	375 mL
1 quart	chilled mixed celery sticks, carrot sticks, green onions and cucumber spears, drained	1 L

Rinse the chicken wings in cool water, and pat completely dry. Combine the corn oil, pepper sauce, vinegar, lemon juice, beer, melted butter and cayenne. Whisk until very smooth. Toss the wings in the sauce, and allow to stand at room temperature 45 minutes while preparing the barbecue.

Heat the barbecue to medium-hot. Lightly oil the grill. Using tongs, remove the wings from the sauce, reserving all liquid in a bowl. Place the wings on the grill, 4 inches (10 cm) above the heat source, and sear quickly on both sides 3-4 minutes. Continue grilling the wings, basting with sauce and turning, until the wings are tender, a rich deep golden brown, and slightly charred at the edges. Total cooking time will be 15-18 minutes. Transfer the wings to a large wooden platter, mounding to serve.

Accompany the wings with a bowl of the blue cheese dressing for dipping, and the ice cold fresh vegetables for munching. Pass plenty of napkins!

Opposite: (On the grill, clockwise from top left) Beach Oysters with Shallot-Butter Sauce (page 62), Herb-Crusted Salmon Fillets (page 73), Swordfish with Pungent Olive Sauce (page 68).

BARBECUED TANDOORI CHICKEN

Tandoori chicken gets its name from the traditional preparation in a tandoor oven, a clay oven used in India that is heated with charcoal or wood. So a barbecue is a wonderful substitute. Let the chicken marinate overnight for the full spicy flavours to develop. Then serve with scented basmati rice, a green salad or steamed green beans, and a selection of chutneys. Serves 4.

4	chicken legs, skinned, about 2 lbs. (1 kg)	4
2	6 oz. (175 g) cartons plain yogourt	2
1	medium onion, peeled and grated	1
1	clove garlic, crushed	1
1 tbsp.	tomato paste	15 mL
1 tbsp.	curry powder	15 mL
2 tsp.	ground turmeric	10 mL
1 tsp.	grated fresh ginger	5 mL
1 tsp.	chili powder	5 mL
1 tsp.	ground coriander	5 mL
1 tsp.	paprika	5 mL
1/2 tsp.	salt	2 mL
	cucumber, tomato and lemon slices for garnish	

In a shallow dish large enough to hold the chicken pieces in a single layer, combine the yogourt, onion, garlic, tomato paste, curry powder, turmeric, ginger, chili powder, coriander, paprika and salt.

Prick the chicken pieces all over with a skewer and place them in the yogourt mixture, turning to coat thoroughly. Cover with plastic wrap and marinate in the refrigerator for 24 hours, turning occasionally.

Heat the barbecue to medium-hot. Remove the chicken from the marinade and thread onto long skewers. Reserve the marinade. Brush the grill with oil and cook the chicken for 45 minutes to 1 hour, depending on the size, turning often so the chicken does not burn. Baste occasionally with the reserved marinade. Lower the heat if necessary during cooking. Arrange the chicken on a warm serving platter and garnish with cucumber, tomato and lemon slices.

TEA-SMOKED GRILLED DUCK

Use your favourite black tea for this unusual creation, or search out the haunting, smokey-flavoured Lapsang Souchong tea from China for a truly unique flavour. Marinate the duck in this Oriental-inspired baste, scatter tea leaves over the coals for added flavour, and serve the same tea iced with lemon as the perfect accompanying beverage. The dish goes beautifully with hot rice and stir-fried snow peas and carrots. Finish with fresh pineapple and a cool sherbet, and don't forget the fortune cookies! Serves 4.

	Far East Marinade (recipe follows)	
2	ducks, quartered	2
1 cup	fresh brewed Lapsang Souchong or other black tea, cooled (reserve tea leaves)	250 mL
1/3 cup	additional dry Lapsang Souchong tea leaves	75 mL
	fresh kumquats or tangerine wedges for garnish	
	fresh citrus leaves	

Prepare the marinade ahead of time, setting aside several hours to blend flavours. Soak the duck quarters in the cooled, infused tea 2 hours to marinate. Drain and add the prepared marinade, toss the duck pieces to coat, and refrigerate 2-3 hours, covered.

Bring the marinated duck pieces to room temperature, uncovered. Heat the barbecue to medium-hot. Lightly oil the grill and scatter the reserved wet and dry tea leaves directly on the coals.

Place the duck quarters on the grill, fat side down, 6 inches (15 cm) above the heat source, and sear 4-5 minutes per side, turning. Begin brushing with the prepared marinade, cover the grill with a lid, and "smoke" the duck until tender, turning frequently, until it is slightly pink on the inside, crispy and slightly charred on the outside — about 15 minutes additional cooking time. Brush the duck once again with the marinade, turn, brush the other side and transfer the duck to a large warmed platter. Allow the duck to rest 8 minutes before serving.

Garnish with kumquats or tangerine wedges and fresh citrus leaves. Spoon any remaining marinade lightly over each portion, and serve the duck hot.

FAR EAST MARINADE

1	10 oz. (225 mL) bottle prepared Hoi Sin sauce (available in the specialty foods department)	1
2 tbsp.	*each* sherry vinegar or white wine vinegar and water	30 mL
1/4 cup	dry sherry	50 mL
4 tbsp.	peanut oil	60 mL
1	clove garlic, crushed	1

In a small saucepan, bring all ingredients to a simmer. Cook 2-3 minutes until bubbly. Remove from heat, and cool.

MEDITERRANEAN SHRIMP-VEGETABLE GRILL

Here is a hearty, satisfying outdoor dinner of grilled shrimp with zucchini, eggplant and stuffed mushrooms, perfect for entertaining. Serve it at room temperature, grilling the vegetables ahead of time and barbecuing the shrimp at the last minute. A summer soup and a fresh berry pie from the in-store bakery are all you need for a summer meal to remember. Serves 4-6.

6	large mushrooms	6
4 tbsp.	cubed mozzarella cheese	60 mL
2 tbsp.	tarragon or other herb vinegar	30 mL
8 tbsp.	olive oil	120 mL
pinch	salt	pinch
pinch	freshly ground black pepper	pinch
pinch	dried tarragon, crumbled	pinch
3	medium zucchini	3
1	small eggplant	1
6	leeks	6
2	medium red bell peppers	2
12	large raw shrimp or prawns, shelled	12

Dressing:

1	egg	1
1	clove garlic, crushed	1
1/3 cup	finely chopped fresh parsley	75 mL
1 tsp.	Dijon mustard	5 mL
1 tbsp.	fresh lemon juice	15 mL
1/2 cup	vegetable oil	125 mL
1	small head red ruffle lettuce for garnish	1

Remove the mushroom stems, reserving the caps. Chop the stems finely and combine with the mozzarella, vinegar, 2 tbsp. (30 mL) of the olive oil, salt, pepper and tarragon. Toss to mix and set aside.

Cut the zucchini and eggplant lengthwise, into 6 slices each. Trim the leeks to 6 inches (15 cm) and halve lengthwise.

Heat the barbecue to hot. Brush the zucchini on both sides with olive oil and grill, turning once, until lightly browned and charred slightly, about 1 minute on each side. Repeat with the eggplant (about 2-3 minutes on each side), the leeks (about 3-4 minutes on each side) and the reserved mushroom caps (about 2-3 minutes on each side). They should have good grill marks on them. Set aside.

Roast the red peppers over high heat or under a hot broiler, turning, until charred all over. Seal in a paper bag and let steam for 5 minutes. Under cold running water, scrape off the charred skin and remove the stem, seeds and membranes. Cut the peppers lengthwise into thin strips. Set aside.

To make the dressing, mix together the egg, garlic, parsley, mustard and lemon juice. Slowly whisk in 4 tbsp. (60 mL) of the remaining olive oil and the vegetable oil. It should be of a thin mayonnaise-like consistency.

Fill the grilled mushroom caps with the mozzarella mixture.

At serving time, heat the barbecue to medium-hot. Line serving plates with lettuce and arrange the grilled vegetables and filled mushroom caps in a decorative pattern.

Grill the shelled shrimp on an oiled grill about 3-4 minutes on each side until just cooked through. They will be bright pink and opaque. They cook quickly and will toughen if left on the grill too long.

Arrange the shrimp over the vegetables. Spoon the dressing over all and serve.

TOMATO-ORANGE GLAZED TIGER SHRIMP

Tiger shrimp are a luxury, well worth the price! Meaty and succulent, they always mean luscious dining. In this recipe they are grilled quickly on a skewer in a nippy orange and tomato-flavoured baste, ready to be served up with additional sauce for dipping, a curly endive salad dressed in a lively vinaigrette, hot wild and white rice and fresh asparagus. Serves 4.

2 tbsp.	*each* butter and corn oil	30 mL
1	small onion, peeled and minced	1
1/3 cup	*each* ketchup and chili sauce	75 mL
1/2 tsp.	*each* chili powder, cinnamon and ground cloves	2 mL
2 tbsp.	*each* soy sauce, brown sugar, honey	30 mL
2 tbsp.	cider vinegar	30 mL
1	medium navel orange, ground (a food processor is fine for this recipe), including rind	1
2 lbs.	jumbo tiger shrimp, shelled and deveined with tails left attached	1 kg
2 cups	cherry tomatoes	500 mL
12	green onions, trimmed to 3 inch (7.5 cm) lengths	12
16	orange slices or wedges (2 oranges)	16
	salt and pepper to taste	

Prepare the basting sauce by heating the butter and oil in a small saucepan over medium-high heat until bubbly. Add the onion, and sauté until softened and pale golden. Add the ketchup, chili sauce, chili powder, cinnamon, cloves, soy sauce, brown sugar, honey, vinegar and ground orange. Heat until bubbly, whisking to combine, and cook 30 minutes over the lowest heat, partially covered, to blend the flavours. The finished sauce should be glossy and the consistency of fruit preserves. Cool to room temperature. Add the prepared shrimp, and marinate 1 hour. Thread the shrimp on skewers, adding whole cherry tomatoes, green onions and orange slices every second or third shrimp.

While the shrimp are marinating, heat the barbecue to medium-hot. Oil the grill, place it 4 inches (10 cm) above the heat source, and sear the skewers on one side 2-3 minutes. Brush with marinade and turn. Sear the other side 2-3 minutes. The shrimp are cooked when they just turn opaque and firm.

Season with salt and pepper and serve sizzling hot, accompanied by any remaining sauce for dipping.

The Easy Gourmet features a photograph of this recipe on page 71.

RILLED RANCH-STYLE TROUT

The secret to this superb grilled trout recipe is simplicity — and a bottle of creamy ranch-style salad dressing! Serve it with grilled summer squash, your favourite leafy green salad and Best-Ever Barbecued Garlic Bread (p. 81). Serves 4.

4	12 oz. (375 g) fresh whole trout, cleaned and gutted	4
	fresh lemon juice	
	salt and pepper to taste	
8 oz.	tiny cooked shrimp	250 g
1/2 cup	fresh bread crumbs	125 mL
4 tbsp.	melted butter	60 mL
2 tbsp.	minced fresh parsley	30 mL
1 tbsp.	*each* minced fresh dill, minced chives	15 mL
	and finely grated lemon rind	
1 cup	bottled Ranch-Style Dressing	250 mL
	lemon wedges, fresh chives and dill for garnish	

Sprinkle the cavities of each trout with lemon juice, salt and pepper. To make the stuffing, toss together the shrimp, bread crumbs, butter, parsley, dill, chives and lemon rind. Divide the stuffing into 4 portions and fill the cavity of each fish. Skewer the trout closed with long wooden skewers.

Heat the barbecue to medium-hot. Oil the grill. Dip the trout into the dressing on both sides. Grill 6 inches (15 cm) above the heat source, until lightly charred and just beginning to flake, about 4-5 minutes per side. Turn once, brushing with additional dressing as the fish cooks.

Arrange the trout on warmed plates and serve at once with lemon wedges, chives and sprigs of fresh dill. Remove the skewers and serve hot.

Note: The trout may be stuffed, skewered, covered loosely with waxed paper and refrigerated up to 6 hours before serving. Bring it to room temperature 20 minutes before cooking.

BEACH OYSTERS WITH SHALLOT-BUTTER SAUCE

When you see fresh oysters in the seafood department, buy up a bushel full, and invite friends over for an authentic "pan roaste." Serve the outdoor-grilled oysters with this lovely shallot-butter sauce, grilled toasted French bread "croutons" and ice-cold beer. Serves 4.

3 dozen	fresh beach oysters, scrubbed	3 dozen
	Savoury Shallot-Butter Sauce	
	(recipe follows)	
	lemon wedges	
1	bottle hot pepper sauce	1

Heat the barbecue to very hot. Oil the grill, and place the oysters directly on it, 3 inches (7.5 cm) above the heat source. Cover with a hood. Smoke the oysters open, about 5 minutes, and serve hot off the grill with a warm pan of Savoury Shallot-Butter Sauce, kept warm right on the barbecue. Offer lemon wedges and a bottle of hot pepper sauce so that guests may season their oysters as they wish.

SAVOURY SHALLOT-BUTTER SAUCE

1/2 lb.	unsalted butter, very cold	250 g
1/3 cup	finely minced shallots	75 mL
3 tbsp.	*each* dry sherry or beer	45 mL
	and cider vinegar	
2 tbsp.	fresh lemon juice	30 mL
pinch	cayenne pepper	pinch
10-12 drops	bottled hot pepper sauce	10-12 drops
2 tbsp.	very finely minced fresh parsley	30 mL
	salt and pepper to taste	

Heat 2 tbsp. (30 mL) of the butter in a saucepan over medium-high heat until bubbly. Add the shallots, and sauté until softened and pale golden, about 5 minutes. Whisk in the sherry, vinegar, lemon juice and cayenne. Heat 2-3 minutes until bubbly and syrupy.

The Easy Gourmet features a photograph of this recipe on page 53.

Cut the remaining cold butter into tablespoons. Over very low heat (barely warm), whisk the cold butter into the sauce, one piece at a time. Add each piece only after the previous piece has melted in. (This is the procedure for preparing a classic beurre blanc, a frothy, creamy butter sauce.) Remove the sauce from the heat and whisk in the hot pepper sauce and parsley. Season lightly with salt and pepper. Serve the sauce just barely warm.

 CALLOP-SHRIMP BUNDLES

For seafood lovers, shrimp and scallops are a knockout combination. In this recipe they are barbecued to steamy, buttery perfection in foil parcels, ready to be tipped out onto individual servings of boiled rice. Accompany this entrée with a crisp steamed vegetable, and watch it disappear! Serves 4.

1/3 cup	butter, at room temperature	75 mL
2	cloves garlic, crushed	2
1 1/2 tbsp.	chopped fresh parsley	20 mL
1 tbsp.	fresh lime juice	15 mL
1/4 tsp.	grated fresh lime peel	1 mL
pinch	cayenne pepper (optional)	pinch
1/2 lb.	fresh shrimp, in the shell	250 g
1/2 lb.	fresh scallops	250 g
	salt and pepper to taste	
4	slices fresh lime	4

In a small bowl, combine the butter, garlic, parsley, lime juice and peel and cayenne pepper, beating well to mix. Set aside.

Shell the shrimp, leaving the tails on. Remove the centre back veins. Cut out 4 squares of heavy foil, each 10 inches (25 cm) square. Divide the shrimp and scallops equally among the 4 squares, placing them in the centre. Sprinkle with salt and pepper. Divide the butter mixture into 4 and place 1 piece in each foil square with a slice of lime. Bring up the sides of each piece of foil to form a parcel and fold over to enclose the contents. Make a small vent in the top of each for air to escape. Heat the barbecue to medium-hot. Cook the parcels 8-10 minutes or until the shrimp and scallops turn opaque. Serve piping hot over fluffy rice.

SPLIT LOBSTER WITH CAJUN MAYONNAISE

Serve this zesty Cajun-flavoured mayonnaise with chilled, cooked lobster halves from the seafood department, or buy fresh, live lobsters from the tanks and have the fish-expert split them live for you to grill at home. (Make sure to grill live lobster within several hours of purchase.) Serve with hot corn-on-the-cob, grilled Beach Oysters (p. 62), crusty bread, and ripe quartered tomatoes. Serves 4.

2	live lobsters, 2 - 2 1/2 lbs. (1-1.25 kg)	2
	each; or	
4	live lobsters, 1 lb. (500 g) each	4
8 tbsp.	melted butter	120 mL
2 tbsp.	vegetable oil	30 mL
	Cajun Mayonnaise (recipe follows)	
	lemon wedges	

Ask the fish-expert to split the lobsters in half, remove the black vein and stomach, and gently crack the large claws.

Heat the barbecue to red-hot. Oil the grill. Combine the melted butter and oil in a small saucepan, and heat on the grill until bubbly. Place the lobsters on the grill, 4 inches (10 cm) from the heat source. Brush with the butter mixture, and cook flesh side down 6-8 minutes, or just until the flesh turns opaque and white. Do not overcook. Brush the cracked claws and flesh during grilling. Turn and grill shell side down 1-2 minutes, brushing the flesh with the butter mixture. The cooked lobster should have a bright red shell.

Remove the lobsters from the grill, and serve sizzling hot, with a crock of chilled Cajun Mayonnaise and lemon wedges.

CAJUN MAYONNAISE

1 1/2 cups	mayonnaise, whisked smooth	375 mL
2	small cloves garlic, crushed	2
1 tsp.	paprika	5 mL
1/2 tsp.	celery salt	2 mL
1/2 tsp.	chili powder	2 mL
pinch	*each* ground cloves and pepper	pinch
1 tbsp.	*each* hot mustard and grainy mustard	15 mL
pinch	sugar	pinch
1 tsp.	bottled hot pepper sauce	5 mL
2 tsp.	fresh lemon juice	10 mL
2 tsp.	finely grated lemon rind	10 mL
1 tbsp.	tomato paste	15 mL

Whisk together all ingredients until smooth. Store the sauce in a glass jar, tightly capped, in the refrigerator until ready to serve. This sauce is best prepared at least 8 hours ahead of time, or the night before. Serve chilled with the hot lobster.

Note: This zesty mayonnaise is good with any type of cold, cooked seafood.

BARBECUED FISH-ON-A-STICK

Grilled fish brochettes are a great way to get children to enjoy seafood —the hot coals make everything taste better, and food done on skewers is fun to eat! Try these succulent seafood skewers with fresh corn-on-the-cob, an enormous fresh fruit salad, hot rice pilaf, and a loaf of crispy garlic bread. Serves 8.

1 lb.	large shrimp, peeled, tails left intact	500 g
1 1/2 lbs.	large scallops	750 g
1 1/2 lbs.	swordfish steaks or other firm fish, cut into 1 inch (2.5 cm) cubes	750 g
18	shucked oysters	18
18	cherry tomatoes	18
2	zucchini, cut into 1 inch (2.5 cm) thick rounds	2
2	*each* red, yellow and green bell peppers, cut into 1 1/2 inch (3.5 cm) squares	2
12	thick slices bacon, cut into 2 inch (5 cm) squares, blanched 2 minutes in simmering water	12
	Seafood Grilling Baste (recipe follows)	
	salt and pepper to taste	
	lemon wedges	
	tartar sauce	

Thread the shrimp, scallops, swordfish and oysters on 8 long skewers, alternating with tomatoes, zucchini and bell peppers, placing bacon slices on either side of the oysters and scallops when threading. Heat the barbecue to medium-hot. Lightly oil the grill.

Brush the prepared skewers with Seafood Grilling Baste, and place on the hot grill, 4 inches (10 cm) from the heat source. Sear 3-4 minutes, turn the skewers, and continue to grill for a total cooking time of about 12-15 minutes. The finished skewers should be a rich golden brown, with slightly charred edges, and the seafood should be just opaque. Do not overcook. Season with salt and pepper to taste.

Remove the skewers from the grill. Serve at once, accompanied by lemon wedges and tartar sauce.

SEAFOOD GRILLING BASTE

8 tbsp.	butter	120 mL
2 tbsp.	Oriental sesame seed oil	30 mL
3 tbsp.	*each* dry sherry, soy sauce and cider vinegar	45 mL
2 tbsp.	brown sugar	30 mL
2	cloves garlic, crushed	2
1 tbsp.	freshly grated ginger	15 mL
2 tbsp.	sharp Chinese-style prepared mustard	30 mL
1/4 cup	honey	50 mL

Combine all ingredients in a small saucepan, and simmer until the mixture is bubbly and the butter is melted. Whisk smooth, cool to room temperature, and set aside until ready to use.

SWORDFISH WITH PUNGENT OLIVE SAUCE

Succulent barbecued swordfish is superb dining with its meaty texture and wonderful flavour. Serve with a mushroom-studded risotto, cherry tomatoes, and a warm baguette. Serves 4.

	Pungent Olive Sauce (recipe follows)	
4	fresh swordfish steaks, 1 inch (2.5 cm) thick	4
	olive oil	
	salt, pepper, dried oregano to taste	

Prepare the sauce and set aside. Brush both sides of the fish with olive oil. Season with salt, pepper and oregano. Marinate 45 minutes.

Heat the barbecue to medium-hot. Oil the grill, place it 4 inches (10 cm) above the heat source, and sear the swordfish 6-7 minutes per side, turning, until the fish is a rich golden brown, crusty on the edges, and just turns opaque. It should just flake easily with a fork. Serve at once topped with sauce.

PUNGENT OLIVE SAUCE

2	cloves garlic, minced	2
1/2 tsp.	salt	2 mL
1/2 cup	fresh parsley, lightly packed	125 mL
1	3 oz. (90 g) jar pimientos, drained	1
3 tbsp.	capers, drained	45 mL
2	anchovy fillets, finely minced	2
1/2 cup	pimiento-stuffed olives, quartered	125 mL
2 tbsp.	*each* brown sugar and sherry vinegar	30 mL
1 tsp.	*each* paprika and black pepper	5 mL
3/4 cup	olive oil	175 mL

In a food processor, process the garlic and salt to a fine paste. Add the parsley and process to a fine mince. Add the pimientos, capers, anchovy and olives, and process to a chunky texture. Add the sugar, vinegar, paprika and pepper and process 2-3 turns. With the motor running, add the olive oil in a thin, steady stream. Serve at room temperature.

The Easy Gourmet features a photograph of this recipe on page 53.

CREOLE-STYLE RED SNAPPER

Snapper is a delicious and versatile fish, and served this way it is unforgettable. Best of all, it can be prepared ahead: simmer up the rich and tangy sauce a day ahead, or even make it days before and keep it in the freezer until just before serving time. To round out this quick, elegant supper, serve steamed fresh peas and pasta salad with vegetables from the deli. Serves 4.

1 lb.	red snapper, cut in 4 pieces	500 g
	vegetable oil	
	salt and pepper to taste	

Creole Sauce:

2 tbsp.	vegetable oil	30 mL
1 tbsp.	butter	15 mL
1	medium onion, finely chopped	1
1	small green bell pepper, cored, seeded and diced	1
1	large clove garlic, crushed	1
1	14 oz. (398 mL) can crushed tomatoes	1
1	2 oz. (57 mL) jar sliced pimientos, drained	1
2 tsp.	*each* sugar and lemon juice	10 mL
1/2 tsp.	*each* chili powder and paprika	2 mL
1/4 tsp.	dry mustard	1 mL
1 tbsp.	chopped fresh parsley	15 mL
	salt and pepper to taste	

To make the sauce, heat the oil and butter in a medium saucepan. Add the onion, pepper and garlic and sauté over medium heat about 5 minutes, until soft but not brown. Stir in the tomatoes, pimientos, sugar, lemon juice, chili, paprika and mustard. Bring to a boil, then reduce the heat to very low and simmer, covered, about 40 minutes until sauce is thickened, stirring occasionally. Stir in the parsley and season to taste with salt and pepper.

Heat the barbecue to medium-hot. Brush the snapper on both sides with oil and season with salt and pepper. Grill 5-6 minutes on each side, turning once, until just firm and cooked.

Place the snapper on a warm serving platter and pour on the heated sauce.

J APANESE EGGPLANT AND GARLIC PLATTER

These savoury (and garlic laden!) Japanese eggplant halves make a delightful side dish to grilled lamb or beef, but are also marvelous tucked into a toasted sourdough bread sandwich with sliced tomatoes, thin slivers of onion, and a slather of mayonnaise. Prepare them several hours ahead of time or overnight, and serve at room temperature for the best flavour. Serves 6.

12	medium-large firm Japanese	12
	eggplants, halved lengthwise	
	salt to taste	
1 1/2 cups	olive oil	375 mL
3 tbsp.	balsamic or red wine vinegar	45 mL
12	large cloves garlic, minced by hand	12
	(essential for this recipe)	
3 tbsp.	*each* finely minced fresh cilantro and	45 mL
	parsley, combined	
	salt and freshly ground black pepper to taste	

Sprinkle the cut sides of the halved eggplants with salt, place them in a colander, and let stand 30 minutes. Pat dry with paper towels.

Place 3 tbsp. (45 mL) of the olive oil in a small non-stick skillet. In a separate container, combine the remaining oil and the vinegar, and marinate the eggplant halves in this mixture 1 hour, turning frequently. Meanwhile, heat the barbecue to medium. Oil the grill, and cook the eggplants slowly, 6 inches (15 cm) above the heat source, turning and brushing, until tender and golden brown, about 20 minutes. Remove from the grill with tongs or a spatula, and lay them out flat on a large platter, side by side.

Meanwhile, heat the reserved olive oil over medium heat and add the garlic. Sauté very gently just until the garlic is soft and the colour very pale (do not burn, or garlic will become bitter). Strew soft, sautéed garlic evenly over the eggplant. Drizzle with any remaining marinade, cilantro and parsley. Season with salt and pepper. Cover the platter with plastic wrap, and allow to marinate and chill several hours before serving. Bring the platter to room temperature for at least 1 hour before serving.

Opposite: (Left to right) Giant Lamb Kebabs with Spicy Tomato Butter (page 20) and Tomato-Orange Glazed Tiger Shrimp (page 60).

HERB-CRUSTED SALMON FILLETS

In this easy, elegant dish, thick salmon fillets are grilled to juicy perfection with a flavourful mayonnaise crust flecked with herbs. Serve with a tender butter lettuce and cucumber salad, hot garlic bread done on the grill, and sliced summer tomatoes. Serves 4.

1 cup	mayonnaise	250 mL
3 tbsp.	snipped fresh dill	45 mL
2 tbsp.	minced fresh parsley	30 mL
2 tbsp.	honey mustard	30 mL
1 tbsp.	fresh lemon juice	15 mL
2 tsp.	finely grated lemon rind	10 mL
1/2 tsp.	paprika	2 mL
4	fresh salmon fillets,	4
	each 6 oz. (180 g)	
	salt and pepper to taste	

Whisk together the mayonnaise, dill, parsley, mustard, lemon juice, lemon rind and paprika. Chill several hours to blend the flavours.

Heat the barbecue to medium-hot. Lightly oil the grill and place it 4 inches (10 cm) above the heat source. Set aside 4 tbsp. (60 mL) of the mayonnaise and chill. Brush 1 tbsp. (15 mL) of the mayonnaise over the skin side of each fillet, and sear the fish 4 minutes on the grill. Brush the uncooked sides with mayonnaise, turn the fillets and sear an additional 3-4 minutes. The salmon is done when it *just* turns opaque and begins to flake easily with a fork. Season with salt and pepper. Serve sizzling hot, each fillet topped with 1 tbsp. (15 mL) of the reserved, chilled mayonnaise. Serve at once.

The Easy Gourmet features a photograph of this recipe on page 53.

PACIFIC STUFFED SALMON

If the west coast has a traditional dish, it has to be salmon. And for summer entertaining a special stuffing, a light creamy sauce and the unique flavour of cooking it over the barbecue give salmon an extra flair. If you wrap the fish in a double sheet of oiled heavy foil for cooking, it won't stick and it will stay beautifully moist. While the salmon cooks, boil up some minted new potatoes and make Herb-Grilled Vegetables (p. 37). Serves 4-6.

Stuffing:

4	slices bacon, finely chopped	4
1	large shallot, finely chopped	1
1	clove garlic, crushed	1
3	mushrooms, finely chopped	3
1 cup	cooked, chopped spinach leaves, well drained (about 7 oz. (200 g) fresh raw spinach)	250 mL
1/2 cup	grated mozzarella cheese	125 mL

1	2 lb. (1 kg) whole fresh salmon, cleaned and scaled, head and tail on	1
	salt and pepper to taste	
	lemon slices for garnish	

Sour Cream Mushroom Sauce:

3 tbsp.	butter	45 mL
2 cups	sliced mushrooms	500 mL
4	green onions, sliced	4
1/2 tsp.	paprika	2 mL
1 cup	light sour cream	250 mL

To make the stuffing, sauté the bacon until crisp in a small saucepan. Remove all but 1 tbsp. (15 mL) of the fat, add the shallot and garlic and sauté about 2 minutes, until soft. Add the mushrooms and lightly sauté about 30 seconds. Remove from heat and mix with the spinach and cheese in a small bowl. Allow to cool.

When the stuffing is cool, sprinkle the inside cavity of the salmon with salt and pepper. Lightly fill with stuffing. Insert six 3 inch (7 cm) metal skewers, 1 1/2 inches (3.5 cm) apart, across the opening of the cavity and close securely by lacing with string. Place the salmon on a double sheet of oiled heavy foil and fold the foil over to enclose the fish, leaving an air opening at the top.

Heat the barbecue to medium-hot. Place the salmon on the barbecue and cook for about 30 minutes, turning once, until the flesh is firm, opaque and just beginning to flake. Allow it to sit, wrapped, for 5 minutes, while you prepare the sauce, then remove the skewers and string and place the salmon on a serving platter. Garnish with lemon slices.

To make the sauce, melt the butter in a medium saucepan. Sauté the mushrooms and green onions, stirring, 1-2 minutes, until slightly soft. Stir in the paprika, then the sour cream. Heat just until the sour cream is warmed through, then pour it into a sauce boat to serve alongside the cooked salmon.

BARBECUED WHOLE SALMON, WEST COAST STYLE

*Barbecued west coast salmon is a summer favourite in British Columbia —
all by itself or as the centre of a warm weather feast. Add hickory chips to the
coals to generate a flavourful smoke. Serves 6-8.*

1	3-4 lb. (1.5-2 kg) whole salmon, cleaned	1
1	stalk chopped fresh parsley	1
1	stalk chopped fresh dill	1
1	onion thinly sliced	1
1	cucumber sliced	1
2	lemons cut into wedges	2
	fresh parsley or watercress for garnish	
	Curry Mayonnaise (recipe follows)	

Heat the barbecue to hot. Season the salmon cavity with parsley, dill and
sliced onion. Wrap the salmon well in heavy foil, using extra foil around the
head and tail to prevent overcooking. With a fork, very lightly press a few
holes in the foil to allow the smoke to add its flavour to the fish.

Cook the fish seam side down for 10 minutes per inch (2.5 cm) of thickness.
Halfway through the cooking time, turn the fish package over. When the
fish is done, slide it onto a large serving platter and pull away as much of
the foil as possible. Gently remove the skin from the back of the head to the
top of the tail. Decorate with sliced cucumber down the centre, and lemon
wedges and parsley or watercress around the outside. Serve with Curry
Mayonnaise.

CURRY MAYONNAISE

Makes 2 cups (500 mL).

1	small onion, finely chopped	1
1	clove garlic, minced	1
2 tbsp.	butter	30 mL
1 tbsp.	curry power or hot curry paste	15 mL
1 tsp.	tomato paste	5 mL
1/2 cup	chicken stock	125 mL
2 tbsp.	orange marmalade	30 mL
1 1/2 cups	mayonnaise	375 mL

Sauté the onion and garlic in the butter until tender. Add curry powder or paste and cook a few minutes longer. Stir in the tomato paste and 4 tbsp. (60 mL) of the chicken stock and cook for 3-4 minutes. Add the marmalade and mix well. Cool and strain. Add the curry liquid to the mayonnaise and add additional chicken stock, if necessary, to thin out the sauce. It should have the consistency of a thick sour cream. Adjust seasoning to taste.

GRILLED MONKFISH WITH LIME BUTTER

Rich, flavourful and inexpensive, monkfish is popularly known as the "poor man's lobster." In this recipe it is grilled Cajun-style, a preparation that works just as well with swordfish and shark. Serve it with Persian Cucumber Salad (p. 116), and Sweet-and-Sour Fruit Kebabs (p. 34). Serves 4.

4	medium monkfish steaks, 1 1/2 - 2 inches (3.5 - 5 cm) thick	4
1	egg, beaten	1
2 tbsp.	Cajun Seasoning (see page 10)	30 mL
	Lime Butter (recipe follows)	

Cut the steaks into serving size pieces and pat dry. Place the beaten egg in a small bowl and mix in the Cajun Seasoning. Dip the fish steaks in the egg mixture. Place them on a rack to dry for a few minutes. Heat the barbecue to medium-hot and grill the prepared steaks 4-5 minutes on each side or until the flesh is opaque when sliced in the centre. Top each steak with 1 tablespoon (15 mL) of Lime Butter.

LIME BUTTER

4 tbsp.	butter, softened	60 mL
	rind of 1 lime, finely chopped	
	juice of 1 lime	

Combine all ingredients thoroughly in a small bowl.

GRILLED STUFFED POTATOES

Grilled baked potatoes are the classic go-with at summer barbecues, and there is almost no limit to the fillings for them. Here are three lively ideas to get you started. Speed up the cooking time by pre-baking the potatoes in the oven. Scrub and prick them with a fork, bake them at 350°F (180°C) for 40 minutes, then wrap them in heavy foil and cook on a medium-hot barbecue for a further 30 minutes, or until soft. Each of these fillings can be prepared ahead, for minimum fuss at serving time.

MEXICAN CHILI FILLING

3 tbsp.	margarine	45 mL
1	small onion, finely chopped	1
1	small green bell pepper, cored, seeded and finely chopped	1
1	clove garlic, crushed	1
2 tsp.	chili powder	10 mL
1	7 oz. (200 mL) can whole kernel corn, drained	1
4	baked potatoes	4
4 tbsp.	milk	60 mL
1 cup	grated Monterey jack cheese	250 mL

Melt the margarine in a small saucepan. Sauté the onion, green pepper and garlic 2-3 minutes until soft but not browned. Stir in the chili powder and sauté 1 minute. Remove from the heat and stir in the corn. Cut each potato in half and scoop out the potato into a medium bowl. Mash with a fork and beat in the milk. Stir in the corn mixture. Spoon the filling back into the potato skins. Sprinkle a little cheese on top of each potato half. Wrap each half loosely in foil and grill for 5 minutes to heat through. Serves 4.

CREAMY SAGE AND ONION FILLING

1 tbsp.	margarine	15 mL
6	green onions, finely chopped	6
2/3 cup	cream cheese, at room temperature	150 mL
1/2 tsp.	dried sage	2 mL
	salt and pepper to taste	
4	baked potatoes	4
4 tbsp.	milk	60 mL

Melt the margarine in a small saucepan and sauté the green onions 1 minute. Combine with the cream cheese, sage, salt and pepper in a small bowl. Cut each potato in half and scoop out the flesh into a medium bowl. Mash with a fork and beat in the milk. Stir in the cream cheese mixture. Spoon the filling back into the potato skins. Wrap each half loosely in foil and grill for 5 minutes to heat through. Serves 4.

CHEESY BACON FILLING

4	slices bacon, finely chopped	4
1	medium onion, finely chopped	1
1 cup	grated Cheddar cheese	250 mL
2 tbsp.	chopped fresh parsley	30 mL
	salt and pepper to taste	
4	baked potatoes	4
4 tbsp.	milk	60 mL

Sauté the bacon in a small saucepan until crisp. Drain it on a paper towel and place it in a small bowl. Add the onion to the bacon fat and sauté 3 minutes, or until soft. Stir the onion into the bacon with the cheese, parsley, salt and pepper. Cut each potato in half and scoop out the potato into a medium bowl. Mash with a fork and beat in the milk. Stir in the bacon and cheese mixture. Spoon the filling back into the potato skins. Wrap each half loosely in foil and grill 5 minutes to heat through. Serves 4.

GRILLED VEGETABLE SALAD

Nowadays there is such an abundant array of fresh vegetables that a platter-salad of grilled fresh vegetables is a must for summertime. Serve this exciting salad at room temperature for the best flavour, with several hot, crispy baguettes and butter served alongside. A pitcher of cold Citrus-Spiced Sun Tea (p. 146) is the ideal beverage. Serves 6-8.

6	small zucchini, halved lengthwise	6
6	small crookneck squash, halved lengthwise	6
6	small pattypan squash, halved crosswise	6
6	small Japanese eggplant, halved lengthwise	6
2	*each* red, yellow, orange and green bell peppers, cut into quarters	2
6	whole carrots, trimmed, with 2 inches (5 cm) stem left attached	6
6	baby leeks, washed and trimmed of root end and toughest green leaves, *or*	6
12	green onions, trimmed	12
6	red potatoes, cut in half	6
2 cups	olive oil	500 mL
2/3 cup	dry white wine or vermouth	150 mL
1/3 cup	white wine vinegar or lemon juice	75 mL
1 tsp.	sugar	5 mL
4	cloves garlic, crushed	4
1/3 cup (1 small bunch)	*each* finely minced fresh rosemary, thyme and oregano	75 mL (1 small bunch)
	salt and freshly ground black pepper to taste	
	sprigs of fresh herbs for garnish	

Wash and trim all vegetables as indicated, and pat completely dry. Whisk together the olive oil, white wine, vinegar, sugar, garlic and herbs until smooth. Place all vegetables in a large roasting pan. Brush on the marinade and toss several times to coat. Marinate at room temperature 1-2 hours.

Meanwhile, heat the barbecue to medium. Oil the grill and cook the vegetables in several batches, 6 inches (15 cm) above the heat source, until just tender-crisp and golden brown in spots, turning once or twice and brushing with marinade. The grilling time for each vegetable may be different. As the cooked vegetables come off the grill, season with salt and pepper and arrange on a large crockery platter. Continue grilling until all vegetables are cooked. Drizzle any remaining marinade over the finished vegetables, and cool to room temperature, at least 1 hour. Garnish with sprigs of fresh herbs and serve.

BEST-EVER BARBECUED GARLIC BREAD

What barbecue feast would be complete without a loaf of hot, buttery garlic bread, right off the grill! Try these variations —all quick, all delicious. Makes 1 loaf (serves 4-6).

1/2 lb.	softened butter	250 g
2-3	cloves garlic, crushed	2-3
2 tbsp.	mixed dried herbs (oregano, thyme, basil, marjoram or dill), *or*	30 mL
6 tbsp.	mixed fresh herbs	90 mL
1/2 tsp.	paprika	2 mL
1	1 lb. (500 g) loaf French or sourdough bread	1

Combine the butter, garlic, herbs and paprika. Slash the bread almost to the bottom in 1 inch (2.5 cm) slices. Spread the butter on the slices, press the loaf to close it and wrap in heavy foil. Grill 6 inches (15 cm) above the heat source for 25 minutes, turning several times, and serve hot.

Herbed Parmesan Loaf: In place of the herbs and paprika, mix 1/3 cup (75 mL) grated Parmesan cheese, 2 tbsp. (30 mL) minced fresh parsley and 1/2 tsp. (2 mL) freshly ground black pepper into the butter.

Lemon-Mustard Loaf: In place of the herbs and paprika, mix 2 tbsp. (30 mL) *each* Dijon mustard and honey mustard, 2 tbsp. (30 mL) minced fresh chives or green onions and 2 tsp. (10 mL) Worcestershire sauce into the butter.

Cajun-Spiced Garlic Loaf: In place of the herbs and paprika, mix 2 tsp. (10 mL) paprika, 1 tsp. (5 mL) each dried thyme, oregano and celery seed, 1 tbsp. (15 mL) bottled hot pepper sauce, and 1 tbsp. (15 mL) apple cider vinegar into the butter.

SALADS

Inspired by the rich summer colours and flavours of Safeway's produce department, this section offers tempting recipes for light main-dish salads from Curry-Spiked Chicken and Fruit Salad to the simple, exotic Gado Gado, and crisp, colourful side salads from Zorba the Greek Salad to Vegetable Medley with Creamy Herb Dip—all guaranteed to perk up summer appetites!

 **ILE-HIGH GRILLED CHICKEN TOSTADAS**

These gorgeous mile-high tostadas are guaranteed to bring sighs of satisfaction! Crispy flour tortillas mounded with refried beans, shredded lettuce, lush tomatoes and green onions, avocado and cilantro-spiked dressing, and the fabulous topping — sizzling slices of grilled chicken hot off the barbecue! Top with sour cream, and serve without waiting. Makes 6.

	Cilantro Fiesta Dressing (recipe follows)	
3	whole boneless chicken breasts, halved, skin attached	3
1 cup	prepared Italian-style vinaigrette	250 mL
6	8 inch (20 cm) flour tortillas	6
	corn oil	
2 cups	canned refried beans, heated to warm	500 mL
	salt, pepper and ground cumin to taste	
3 cups	finely shredded chilled iceberg lettuce	750 mL
2 cups	diced ripe tomatoes	500 mL
2 bunches	green onions, thinly sliced	2 bunches
2	avocados, diced	2
1 cup	sour cream, whisked smooth	250 mL
	fresh cilantro sprigs for garnish	

Prepare the Cilantro Fiesta Dressing several hours in advance, or overnight, to blend the flavours. Marinate the chicken breast halves in the vinaigrette several hours or overnight.

Bring the chicken to room temperature for 1 hour while preparing the barbecue. Heat the barbecue to medium-hot and oil the grill.

Meanwhile, fry each tortilla in 1/2 inch (1 cm) hot corn oil until crispy and puffy, about 1 minute per side. Drain on brown paper, and set aside. Heat the refried beans gently and keep warm, covered.

Grill the chicken 4 inches (10 cm) above the heat source, 6-7 minutes per side, turning twice and brushing with the marinade. After the initial searing, season on both sides with salt, pepper and ground cumin. The finished chicken should be a rich golden brown, slightly charred on the edges, and juicy inside. Remove the chicken to a carving board, and allow to rest 10 minutes before carving.

While the chicken cooks, assemble the tostadas. Place each crisp tortilla on a festive plate. Divide the warm beans among the tortillas, spreading them to within 1 inch (2.5 cm) of the outside edge. Mound with shredded lettuce, scatter on diced tomatoes, green onions and avocado. Slice the grilled chicken on the diagonal into 1/4 inch (5 mm) wide strips, and place 1 sliced breast on top of each tostada. Drizzle with Cilantro Fiesta Dressing, top with a generous spoonful of sour cream and garnish with cilantro sprigs.

CILANTRO FIESTA DRESSING

1 tsp.	salt	5 mL
1	large clove garlic, minced	1
1/3 cup	pine nuts, toasted in a 325°F (160°C) oven 7-8 minutes until golden, and cooled	75 mL
1 cup	fresh cilantro, lightly packed	250 mL
1 cup	fresh parsley sprigs, lightly packed	250 mL
3 tbsp.	sherry vinegar or white wine vinegar	45 mL
1 tsp.	chili powder	5 mL
1/2 tsp.	sugar	2 mL
1 1/4 cups	olive oil	300 mL

In a food processor fitted with a steel blade, process the salt and garlic to a fine paste. Add the pine nuts, and process to a paste. Add the cilantro and parsley, and process until finely minced. Add the vinegar, chili and sugar. With the motor running, add the oil in a thin, steady stream until smooth. Transfer the dressing to a glass jar and chill until ready to use.

The Easy Gourmet features a photograph of this recipe on page 89.

MEXICAN FIESTA TACO SALAD

This savoury party salad is adored by kids and teenagers, and is a great choice for a backyard summer party. It's everything you want in a summer salad: a snap to make, fun to eat, and inexpensive. Best of all, it's a good nutritious meal all by itself. Serve it with a pitcher of Non-Alcoholic Summer Sangria (p. 142) or ice-cold beer for the grown-ups. Serves 4-6.

1 lb.	lean ground beef	500 g
3 tbsp.	corn oil	45 mL
1	large onion, diced	1
1	green bell pepper, diced	1
1	14 oz. (398 mL) can red kidney beans, drained and rinsed	1
1	7 1/2 oz. (213 mL) can tomato sauce	1
1	1 oz. (35 g) pkg. Taco Seasoning mix	1
1	head chilled iceberg lettuce, shredded	1
3	firm, ripe tomatoes, cut into large dice	3
1	small cucumber, thinly sliced	1
1	bunch green onions, thinly sliced	1
1	red onion, diced	1
2	avocados, diced	2
1/2 lb.	shredded sharp Cheddar cheese	250 g
1	8 oz. (250 g) bag corn tortilla chips	1
1 cup	sliced black ripe olives, pitted	250 mL
2 cups	fresh red salsa (available in the deli department)	500 mL
1	6 oz. (170 g) container avocado guacamole (available in the frozen food section), thawed and chilled	1

Sauté the ground beef until the meat is no longer pink, and is crumbled and browned. Drain off all fat. Set aside.

Heat the oil in a large skillet over medium-high heat, and sauté the onion and bell pepper 7-8 minutes until softened and pale golden in colour. Add the browned meat, kidney beans, tomato sauce and seasoning mix. Bring the mixture to a simmer, and cook 12 minutes, stirring frequently. The mixture should be glossy and thickened. Set aside, and keep just barely warm.

To assemble the salad: In a very large wooden or crockery salad bowl, layer the meat-bean mixture, lettuce, tomatoes, cucumber, green onions, red onion, avocado, cheese, tortilla chips and olives. Bring to the table, toss gently to combine, and serve each portion mounded on a large dinner plate.

Pass a bowl of chilled red salsa and a bowl of chilled guacamole to top each portion, as desired.

SUMMER CILANTRO-SPIKED DRESSING

This delectable cilantro-flecked dressing is wonderful on fresh vegetable salads, chicken salads with crisp greens, taco salads, or any tossed salad accompanying Mexican-inspired grilled entrées. Makes 2 cups (500 mL).

1	clove garlic, minced	1
1 tsp.	salt	5 mL
1 cup	*each* packed cilantro and fresh parsley	250 mL
1/4 cup	sherry vinegar, cider vinegar *or* red wine vinegar	50 mL
3/4 cup	olive oil	175 mL
1/4 tsp.	bottled hot pepper sauce	1 mL
pinch	sugar	pinch

In a food processor fitted with a steel blade, process the garlic and salt to a paste. Add the cilantro and parsley, and process to a fine mince. Add the vinegar and process 10 seconds. With the motor running, add the olive oil in a thin, steady stream. Add hot pepper sauce and sugar to taste. Chill the dressing several hours or overnight in a glass jar with a tight lid, and whisk smooth before using.

THE GREAT CAESAR

This delightful version of a Caesar salad makes entertaining a snap. The dressing is prepared ahead of time and the oversize croutons add a classy touch. Serve it with a loaf of hot garlic bread or sourdough, and enjoy! For a main course, top each serving with a generous portion of lump crab meat or shrimp. Serves 4-6.

3/4 cup	olive oil	175 mL
4 tbsp.	fresh lemon juice	60 mL
1/2 tsp.	sugar	2 mL
1	egg, lightly beaten	1
2/3 cup	freshly grated Parmesan cheese	150 mL
1 tbsp.	Dijon mustard	15 mL
1	large clove garlic, crushed	1
1/2 tsp.	*each* Worcestershire sauce, salt and black pepper	2 mL
2	anchovy fillets, mashed to a paste	2
2	heads romaine lettuce, outer leaves discarded, rinsed and dried; well chilled	2
2 cups	Home-Style Croutons (recipe follows)	500 mL
	freshly ground black pepper to taste	

Prepare the dressing by whisking together the olive oil, lemon juice, sugar, egg, 1/3 cup (75 mL) of the Parmesan cheese, mustard, garlic, Worcestershire sauce, salt, pepper and mashed anchovy. The dressing should be emulsified, creamy and medium-thick. Chill in a tightly-capped glass jar several hours before using. Shake well before dressing salad.

To assemble the salad, cut or tear the chilled romaine lettuce into generous pieces. Toss with the prepared dressing to coat the leaves. Add the remaining 1/3 cup (75 mL) Parmesan cheese and the Home-Style Croutons. Serve at once on large chilled plates. Pass the pepper grinder!

The Easy Gourmet features a photograph of this recipe on front cover.

HOME-STYLE CROUTONS

1/2 cup	olive oil	125 mL
2 cups	crustless day-old firm French or white bread, cut into 1 inch (2.5 cm) cubes	500 mL
	seasoned garlic salt (with parsley and herb flecks)	

Heat the olive oil in a large non-stick skillet over medium heat. Add the bread cubes, and toss quickly to coat. Sauté croutons 3-5 minutes, stirring, until pale golden brown and crispy. Remove from heat, and toss lightly with garlic salt. Serve within several hours of preparation.

VEGETABLE MEDLEY WITH CREAMY HERB DIP

For a change of pace from salad, try this gorgeous vegetable platter, a tasty and healthful complement to any grilled meat or fish. Look for red, green, yellow and orange peppers, cucumber, broccoli, cauliflower, carrots, zucchini, cherry tomatoes, and other vegetables that add to the cornucopia of colours. There is such a wide summertime selection in the produce department that you will only need a few of each vegetable. Wash and chill them early in the day, so they are crisp and cold, ready to pop into a basket lined with greens, or on a wooden platter, and serve with dip on the side. Makes 1 cup (250 mL).

1/2 cup	mayonnaise	125 mL
1/2 cup	thick sour cream	125 mL
3 tbsp.	chopped fresh herbs such as dill, parsley, basil, oregano, tarragon	45 mL
1 tbsp.	Worcestershire sauce	15 mL
2	green onions, finely chopped	2
3 drops	bottled hot pepper sauce, or to taste	3 drops
	salt and pepper to taste	

Gently mix together all the ingredients and chill until serving time. The dip will keep, refrigerated, for 3 days.

The Easy Gourmet features a photograph of this recipe on page 125.

IZZA SALAD

Here is the kind of recipe you can experiment with. Feta cheese, artichoke hearts and pine nuts add a sophisticated touch, but the combinations of cheeses, vegetables and meats you can use are endless. So make meal times fun — set out a variety of toppings and let everyone design their own pizza salad. Serves 4.

1	ripe avocado, peeled and seeded	1
1/2 cup	sour cream	125 mL
1	large tomato, very finely chopped	1
2	green onions, very finely chopped	2
	salt and pepper to taste	
	lettuce leaves	
4	pita breads, 7 inches (18 cm) in diameter	4
1	small red bell pepper, cored, seeded and sliced thin	1
1 cup	crumbled feta cheese	250 mL
1	3 oz. (100 g) pkg. pepperoni sticks, sliced	1
1	6 1/2 oz. (184 mL) jar marinated artichoke hearts	1
4 tbsp.	toasted pine nuts	60 mL

In a small bowl, mash the avocado and stir in the sour cream, tomato and green onions. Season to taste with salt and pepper.

Place 1 or 2 lettuce leaves over each pita bread, just to cover. Divide the avocado mixture among the pita breads, spreading it over the lettuce. Sprinkle the red pepper, cheese and pepperoni on top. Remove the artichoke hearts from the marinade, reserving the marinade. Cut any larger ones in half. Divide among the pita breads and sprinkle with pine nuts. Drizzle 1 tbsp. (15 mL) of reserved marinade over the topping on each pita, and serve.

Opposite: (Top to bottom) Non-Alcoholic Summer Sangria (page 142), Mile-High Grilled Chicken Tostadas (page 82).

PASTA AND SUMMER PEPPERS SALAD

In days gone by, a bell pepper meant only one thing — a bright green beauty. Nowadays, the produce department boasts a cornucopia of fresh, vibrant, rainbow-hued peppers: brilliant reds, oranges, yellow, even purple! Try this gorgeous combination of peppers tossed with fusilli pasta, and serve it with grilled Italian sausages, a great loaf of crusty bread, and red wine. Serves 6.

1 lb.	dried fusilli pasta (coils)	500 g
3/4 cup	olive oil	175 mL
2	*each* red, orange, yellow and green bell peppers, stemmed, seeded and cut into thin julienne strips	2
1	onion, cut into thin slivers	1
3	cloves garlic, slivered	3
2 tbsp.	*each* sugar and balsamic or red wine vinegar	30 mL
1 tbsp.	dried fennel seeds, crushed	15 mL
1/2 cup	fresh basil, stacked and cut crosswise into thin chiffonade (ribbons)	125 mL
1/2 cup	pine nuts, toasted in a 325°F (160°C) oven 7-8 minutes until golden, and cooled	125 mL
	salt and black pepper to taste	

Cook the pasta al dente (firm to the bite) in boiling water with 1 tbsp. (15 mL) each salt and olive oil. Drain, rinse briefly in cool water, and drain again. Toss with 1 tbsp. (15 mL) olive oil to loosen. Set aside.

Heat 4-5 tbsp. (60-75 mL) of the olive oil in a large wok over medium-high heat. Add the peppers, and stir-fry quickly until tender-crisp and lightly coloured. Add the peppers to the pasta, and toss to combine. Add 2 tbsp. (30 mL) of the olive oil to the wok, and add the slivered onion. Stir-fry 5-6 minutes, until the onion is softened and pale golden. Add the garlic, sugar and vinegar to the onions, and sauté 1-2 minutes until glossy and bubbly. Add the fennel, heat 30 seconds, and remove from heat. Add the contents of the wok to the pasta and peppers, along with the remaining olive oil, the basil and pine nuts. Toss, taste for salt and pepper, and set aside 2-3 hours to allow the flavours to blend. Serve the salad cool or at room temperature.

The Easy Gourmet features a photograph of this recipe on page 107.

GADO GADO

Gado literally means "to sample," which describes perfectly the way this potpourri of vegetables is served and enjoyed. It is a meatless mixed vegetable salad, served with individual dipping bowls of spicy peanut sauce, or presented appetizer-style on a large platter with a bowl of sauce in the centre. In Indonesia—the home of this dish—salads can be hot dishes as well as cool. The shrimp crackers are a wonderful change of pace. Look for them in the specialty foods section. Serves 4.

1	3 oz. (100 g) box shrimp crackers	1

Peanut Sauce:

1/3 cup	unsweetened fine coconut	75 mL
1 1/2 cups	boiling water	375 mL
1 1/2 tbsp.	vegetable oil	20 mL
2	shallots, finely chopped	2
2	cloves garlic, crushed	2
1/2 cup	chunky peanut butter	125 mL
1 1/2 tbsp.	brown sugar	20 mL
1 tbsp.	soy sauce	15 mL
1 tbsp.	lemon juice	15 mL
1 tsp.	chili powder	5 mL
4 tbsp.	half-and-half cream	60 mL

Salad:

2	potatoes, peeled and sliced	2
1 1/2 cups	sliced green beans (about 4 oz. (125 g))	375 mL
4 cups	packed spinach leaves, stems removed	1 L
2 cups	fresh bean sprouts (about 2 oz. (50 g))	500 mL
4	hard-cooked eggs, shelled, cut in wedges	4
1/2 cup	sliced cucumber	125 mL

Prepare the shrimp crackers according to package directions.

To make the sauce, place the coconut in a large measuring jug or bowl. Pour the boiling water over it and let stand 15 minutes. Strain it into a bowl through a fine sieve, pressing out all the liquid. Set the liquid aside and discard the coconut.

In a medium saucepan, heat the oil and sauté the shallots and garlic over medium heat for about 3 minutes, until soft but not brown. Stir in the coconut liquid, peanut butter, sugar, soy sauce, lemon juice and chili powder. Bring to a boil, stirring, then turn the heat to low and simmer 10 minutes until thickened. Stir in the cream and simmer 3 minutes longer. Remove from the heat and set aside.

To make the salad, steam the potatoes for 10 minutes and keep warm. Steam the beans for 5 minutes or until tender-crisp, and keep warm. Cook the spinach in a small amount of boiling water for 30 seconds. Strain, pressing out excess water, and keep warm. Steam the bean sprouts for 30 seconds and keep warm. Heat the peanut sauce.

Set out 4 dinner plates. Place a small bowl or ramekin dish of the peanut sauce in the centre of each one. Around the bowl, arrange small piles of potato slices, beans, hard-cooked eggs, cucumber, shrimp crackers, spinach and bean sprouts. Serve immediately.

The Easy Gourmet features a photograph of this recipe on page 125.

ZORBA THE GREEK SALAD

Everyone loves Greek salad with its festive, colourful mix of crisp bell peppers, bright red tomatoes, cooling cucumber, zesty onion, tangy feta cheese and Greek olives. Dressed in an herby vinaigrette, this main-course salad needs only warm pita bread or crusty French bread as an accompaniment. If the salad is part of a larger meal, serve sizzling Giant Lamb Kebabs (p. 20) and roasted potatoes. Serves 4-6.

	Greek Salad Vinaigrette (recipe follows)	
6	firm, ripe tomatoes, cut into 1 inch (2.5 cm) chunks	6
1	large onion, coarsely diced	1
2	long English cucumbers, cut into 1/2 inch (1 cm) cubes, peels left on	2
2	*each* green and red bell peppers, stemmed, seeded and cut into 1/2 inch (1 cm) squares	2
6-8 oz.	feta cheese, coarsely crumbled	180-250 g
1/2 cup	Greek Kalamata olives (from the deli department)	125 mL
4 tbsp.	minced fresh mint leaves or parsley	60 mL

Prepare the dressing, and set aside several hours to blend the flavours.

To assemble the salad, gently toss together the prepared tomatoes, onion, cucumber, and peppers. Mound the mixture on a large oval crockery platter. Whisk the dressing to combine, and pour over the salad. Top with crumbled cheese and scatter olives over the salad. Sprinkle the salad with the minced mint. Serve cool or at room temperature.

GREEK SALAD VINAIGRETTE

1	large clove garlic, minced	1
1 tsp.	salt	5 mL
1	small bunch fresh mint leaves, lightly packed (about 1/2 cup (125 mL))	1
2 tbsp.	dried oregano	30 mL
1 tbsp.	dried thyme	15 mL
1 tsp.	sugar	5 mL
3/4 cup	fruity extra-virgin olive oil	175 mL
1/4 cup	red wine vinegar	50 mL

In a food processor fitted with a steel blade, process the garlic and salt to a paste. Add the mint leaves, and process to a fine mince. Add the oregano, thyme, and sugar and process smooth. With the motor running, add the olive oil in a thin, steady stream. Add the vinegar. Taste and correct for seasonings. Transfer the dressing to a glass jar, cap tightly, and store in a cool place several hours. Bring the dressing to room temperature before using, shaking the jar vigorously to blend before using.

The Easy Gourmet features a photograph of this recipe on page 107.

PASTA E FAGIOLI SALAD

This salad, whose name means "pasta and beans," is a complete balanced meal, hearty enough to satisfy with nothing more than a great loaf of Italian bread and some crisp greens. For dessert, serve a basket of summer fruits, a glass bowl of ice-water to rinse them in, and assorted Italian cheeses. Serves 6.

	Pasta Salad Dressing (recipe follows)	
1 lb.	short tube-shaped pasta (penne or ziti)	500 g
2 cups	cooked white beans (great northern), drained	500 mL
1 cup	pepperoni, very thinly sliced into rounds	250 mL
1 cup	*each* thinly sliced celery and red onion	250 mL
1	*each* red and yellow bell pepper, thinly sliced	1
1 cup	sliced black olives, pitted	250 mL
1/4 cup	minced fresh parsley	50 mL
1 cup	freshly grated Parmesan cheese	250 mL

Prepare the Pasta Salad Dressing several hours in advance to allow the flavours to blend.

Cook the pasta al dente (firm to the bite) in boiling water with 1 tbsp. (15 mL) each salt and olive oil added. Drain at once, and rinse with cool water to stop the cooking.

Toss together the barely warm pasta, drained and rinsed beans, pepperoni, celery, red onion, bell peppers and olives. Whisk the prepared dressing smooth, and pour it over the salad. Toss gently with your hands or a rubber spatula to coat the ingredients thoroughly. Cover and chill the salad overnight for the best flavours. Bring to room temperature before serving.

To serve, mound the salad on a festive crockery platter, sprinkle with the minced parsley, and pass a bowl of Parmesan.

PASTA SALAD DRESSING

2 tsp.	salt	10 mL
2	cloves garlic, minced	2
2	4 1/2 oz. (128 mL) bottles pimientos or roasted red peppers, drained	2
1 tbsp.	*each* Parmesan cheese and brown sugar	15 mL
1/4 cup	balsamic vinegar or red wine vinegar	50 mL
3/4 cup	olive oil	175 mL
	freshly ground black pepper to taste	

In a food processor fitted with a steel blade, process the salt and garlic to a fine paste, scraping sides down. Add the drained pimiento and process to a smooth purée. Add the Parmesan, sugar and vinegar, and process several seconds to blend. With the motor running, add the olive oil in a thin, steady stream until blended. Season with liberal grindings of black pepper. Set the dressing aside several hours to blend the flavours before dressing the salad. Do not chill, or the dressing will thicken.

CURRY-SPIKED CHICKEN AND FRUIT SALAD

This delightful summer salad is an excellent choice for a backyard summer luncheon, bridal shower, or summer tea. Chock full of chicken and seasonal summer fruits, the whole works is bound with a creamy curry-spiked dressing. Scatter fresh berries over the salad for a casual yet festive presentation, and accompany with tiny hot brioche and butter curls, cool fresh tiny asparagus spears, carrot salad, and a decadent chocolate dessert. Serves 8.

	Curry Cream Dressing (recipe follows)	
4 cups	cooked chicken, coarsely cubed or shredded	1 L
2 cups	thinly sliced celery	500 mL
1/2 cup	*each* thinly sliced green onions and diced red onion	125 mL
2 cups	red seedless grapes	500 mL
1 cup	green seedless grapes, halved	250 mL
2 cups	diced seasonal melon (cantaloupe, honeydew or Persian) in 1/2 inch (1 cm) cubes	500 mL
2	10 oz. (284 mL) cans mandarin oranges, drained	2
2	tart green apples, coarsely diced	2
1	large papaya (firm yet ripe), coarsely diced	1
1	*each* red and yellow bell pepper, diced	1
1 cup	slivered almonds, toasted in a 325°F (160°C) oven 8 minutes until golden	250 mL
	crisp greens	
	garnishes: tiny clusters of red seedless grapes, whole raspberries and strawberries, melon balls, kiwi slices	

Prepare the dressing 1-2 hours ahead of time (or overnight) to allow the flavours to blend.

Gently combine the chicken, celery, green and red onion, red and green grapes, melon, oranges, apples, papaya and bell peppers, mixing thoroughly. Whisk the prepared dressing smooth and pour over the chicken and fruits. Fold the dressing in gently to combine. Finally, fold in the toasted almonds, cover the salad with plastic wrap and chill several hours for the flavours to blend.

To serve, line a glass bowl or platter with crisp greens. Mound salad on the platter and garnish with tiny clusters of grapes and melon balls, and scatter with berries and kiwi slices. Serve this salad chilled or cool for the best flavour.

CURRY CREAM DRESSING

2/3 cup	sour cream or yogourt	150 mL
2/3 cup	mayonnaise	150 mL
1 tbsp.	curry powder	15 mL
2 tbsp.	honey	30 mL
1/3 cup	chutney, puréed	75 mL
1 tbsp.	finely grated lemon rind	15 mL
2 tbsp.	fresh lemon juice	30 mL
pinch	cayenne pepper	pinch
	salt and freshly ground black pepper to taste	

Whisk smooth the sour cream and mayonnaise. Add the curry powder, honey, chutney, lemon rind, lemon juice, cayenne and salt and pepper to taste. Whisk smooth, taste and correct for seasonings. Chill the dressing, covered, several hours or overnight before using.

DELI "WURST SALAT" BAVARIAN-STYLE

The Swiss and Germans love salads featuring sausages and franks, with good reason. They are delicious and need only a nice loaf of freshly-baked bread to complete the feast. Try your own combination of favourite deli meats! Serves 6.

1 1/2 lbs.	deli franks or cooked sausages (Bavarian smokies, franks, cervelat, kielbasa, or a combination)	750 g
2 lbs.	new potatoes (red or white)	1 kg
1/2 cup	sliced sweet gherkin pickles	125 mL
1/3 cup	sliced dill pickles	75 mL
1	small red onion, thinly sliced	1
3 tbsp.	white wine vinegar	45 mL
2/3 cup	*each* sour cream and mayonnaise, whisked smooth	150 mL
2 tbsp.	grainy mustard	30 mL
1 tbsp.	Dijon mustard	15 mL
2 tbsp.	whole mustard seed	30 mL
1 tbsp.	brown sugar, packed	15 mL
	salt and freshly ground black pepper to taste	
	crisp escarole or leaf lettuce	
3	hard-cooked eggs, sliced or finely chopped	3

Simmer the sausages 2 minutes to heat through. Remove and drain. Cool to room temperature. Slice into 1/4 inch (5 mm) thick rounds and place in a deep crockery or porcelain bowl.

Meanwhile, cook the potatoes in boiling salted water until firm-tender, about 10-12 minutes. Drain and cool completely. Slice 1/2 inch (1 cm) thick. Toss with the sausages. Add the sweet and dill pickles and onion.

Whisk together the vinegar, sour cream, mayonnaise, mustards, mustard seed, and brown sugar. Season to taste with salt and black pepper. Pour the dressing over the ingredients in the bowl, and toss gently. Adjust seasonings to taste. Cover and chill several hours or overnight. To serve, bring to room temperature and mound the salad in a bowl lined with crispy escarole or leaf lettuce. Garnish with hard-cooked eggs.

S WEET CORN AND PEPPER SALAD

Microwave cooking will ensure that the vegetables for this salad retain their bright, natural colour — the most attractive feature of this dish. Prepare it ahead and serve it chilled on crisp lettuce, with steaks, chops, fish, or chicken from the barbecue. Serves 4-6.

4	large ears corn	4
1	red bell pepper	1
1	green bell pepper	1
1	small sweet onion	1

Vinaigrette:

2 tbsp.	white wine vinegar	30 mL
1 tbsp.	sugar or honey	15 mL
4 tbsp.	olive oil	60 mL
4 tbsp.	chopped fresh parsley	60 mL
1 tsp.	chopped fresh basil or tarragon	5 mL
	salt to taste	
	freshly ground black pepper to taste	
	lettuce leaves for garnish	

Cut silk and stalk ends off the corn, leaving husk intact. Arrange the ears "bicycle-spoke" fashion in the microwave with the stalk ends towards the outside. Microwave on HIGH 100% power 8-10 minutes until kernels are cooked, turning each ear over halfway through the cooking time. Allow to cool in the husks and then cut off the kernels with a very sharp knife. Wash and seed the peppers. Peel the onion. Cut the peppers and onion into 1/4 inch (5 mm) dice. Place in a microproof dish, cover and microwave on HIGH 100% power 2 minutes until tender-crisp, stirring halfway through the cooking time. Allow to cool and mix with the corn kernels. Cover and chill.

To make the vinaigrette, place the vinegar and sugar or honey in a glass jam jar. Microwave, uncovered, on MEDIUM LOW 30% power 1 - 1 1/2 minutes until the sugar or honey is dissolved. Allow to cool and then add the remaining ingredients. Cover the jar, shake vigorously and chill. At serving time, toss the vegetables with the vinaigrette. To serve, line a dish with lettuce leaves and arrange the salad on top.

The Easy Gourmet features a photograph of this recipe on page 107.

CHINATOWN MAPLE CHICKEN SALAD

This is one of those recipes where cultures unite. Chinese soy sauce and Canadian maple syrup blend together in the dressing, and water chestnuts from the east are tossed with western Canadian peaches in the salad. A fresh, unusual blend and a satisfying lunch or light patio supper with a simple rice salad. Serves 4.

2	whole boneless chicken breasts, about 1 lb. (500 g)	2
8 oz.	green beans, cut in 2 inch (5 cm) slices, about 2 cups (500 mL)	250 g
4 oz.	snow peas, trimmed	125 g
2	peaches, peeled, pitted and sliced	2
1	7 oz. (227 g) can sliced water chestnuts, drained	1
4 tbsp.	vegetable oil	60 mL
3 tbsp.	tamari or soy sauce	45 mL
2 tbsp.	maple syrup	30 mL
2 tbsp.	lemon juice	30 mL
1 tbsp.	white wine vinegar	15 mL
4 tbsp.	slivered toasted almonds	60 mL

Place the chicken breasts, skin side up, in a large skillet and pour in enough water to almost cover. Cover the skillet and poach over low heat until cooked, about 30 minutes. With a slotted spoon, remove the chicken from the water, cool slightly, then cover and refrigerate until completely chilled.

Meanwhile, steam the beans for 5 minutes, until still slightly crisp. Cool them in a sieve under cold running water. Steam the snow peas for 3 minutes. Cool the same way. Drain the beans and snow peas well, and toss them with the peaches and water chestnuts in a large bowl. Set aside.

To make the dressing, beat together the oil, tamari or soy sauce, maple syrup, lemon juice and vinegar. When the chicken is completely cool, remove the skin and cut each breast in half. Cut the chicken into 1/4 inch (5 mm) thick slices. Place the bean mixture in a shallow serving dish and arrange the chicken slices, overlapping, on top. Pour on the dressing and sprinkle with the almonds.

INDONESIAN SHRIMP AND RICE SALAD

Tamari, a subtle-tasting soy sauce, gives this salad a delicate, Oriental flavour. Served with generous slices of granary bread, the salad makes an exotic lunch or supper. You can also prepare it without the shrimp and offer it as an unusual accompaniment to barbecue or other meat dishes. Serves 4.

3/4 cup	raw brown rice, cooked and cooled	175 mL
4 oz.	shelled, cooked shrimp	125 g
3	green onions, diagonally sliced	3
2 cups	fresh bean sprouts	500 mL
1 cup	toasted cashews	250 mL
1/2 cup	currants	125 mL
1	small red bell pepper, cored, seeded, and thinly sliced	1
2 tbsp.	toasted sesame seeds	30 mL

Tamari-Nut Dressing:

4 tbsp.	vegetable oil	60 mL
2 tbsp.	tamari sauce	30 mL
2 tbsp.	smooth peanut butter	30 mL
1 tbsp.	lemon juice	15 mL
1 tbsp.	wine vinegar	15 mL
1	clove garlic, crushed	1
2 tsp.	honey	10 mL
1 tsp.	curry powder	5 mL
1/4 tsp.	ground ginger	1 mL
pinch	black pepper	pinch

In a large bowl combine the rice, shrimp, onions, bean sprouts, cashews, currants, red bell pepper and sesame seeds. Make the dressing in a separate bowl or measuring jug. Beat together the oil, tamari sauce, peanut butter, lemon juice, vinegar, garlic, honey, curry powder, ginger and pepper. Pour the dressing over the salad and toss to combine well. Cover and marinate in the refrigerator 30 minutes to 1 hour before serving.

MINTED LENTIL AND CHICK PEA SALAD

Rich in protein, minerals and iron, lentils are the perfect light and nourishing hot weather food. The green lentil is particularly good for salads, as it holds its shape beautifully. With a chilled puréed soup and warm garlic bread, this salad makes an excellent summer meal. Serves 4.

1/2 cup	green lentils	125 mL
2	cloves garlic, split in half	2
1	bay leaf	1
1	14 oz. (398 mL) can chick peas, drained	1
1 cup	lightly packed parsley, chopped	250 mL
1 cup	lightly packed mint, chopped	250 mL
1	medium red onion, coarsely chopped	1
2	medium tomatoes, seeded and coarsely chopped	2
1/2	long English cucumber, sliced and quartered	1/2
4 tbsp.	vegetable oil	60 mL
4 tbsp.	olive oil	60 mL
3 tbsp.	lemon juice	45 mL
	salt and freshly ground black pepper to taste	
	crisp curly lettuce leaves	

Place the lentils, garlic and bay leaf in a medium saucepan and add enough water to cover by 1 inch (2.5 cm). Bring to a boil, reduce the heat and simmer until the lentils are tender, about 15-20 minutes. Drain. Discard the garlic and bay leaf. Place the lentil mixture in a medium salad bowl and add the chick peas, parsley and mint. Toss together. Cool. Add the onion, tomato and cucumber.

In a small bowl, whisk together the oils and lemon juice. (The dressing will be tart.) Stir the dressing into the salad. Add salt and pepper to taste.

Serve chilled on a bed of curly lettuce.

HERBED AVOCADO-PROSCIUTTO SALAD

Delicately cured prosciutto and smooth mozzarella bring the sensuous flavours of Italy to this salad. Have your deli department slice the ham wafer thin for wrapping around the avocado wedges, then pick up some fresh croissants or poppy seed rolls at the in-store bakery. Or serve the prosciutto-wrapped avocado on its own for a wonderful starter salad. Serves 4.

2	ripe avocados, peeled, pitted and halved	2
12	thin slices prosciutto	12
2	large tomatoes, cored and sliced	2
8	slices mozzarella cheese	8

Garlic-Herb Dressing:

6 tbsp.	olive oil	90 mL
7 tsp.	fresh lemon juice	35 mL
1	large clove garlic, crushed	1
2 tbsp.	chopped fresh parsley or chives	30 mL
	salt and pepper to taste	

Cut each avocado half into 3 wedges. Wrap a slice of prosciutto around each wedge. Arrange 3 wedges on each of 4 plates in a fan shape. Arrange alternate overlapping slices of tomato and mozzarella cheese in a semi-circle around the avocado wedges.

To make the dressing, beat the olive oil and lemon juice in a small bowl until well mixed. Stir in the garlic, parsley or chives, salt and pepper. Spoon the dressing over all and serve at once.

FRENCH POTATO SALAD WITH SHALLOTS

Try this zesty southern French potato salad, reminiscent of the Provençal hillside full of lush wild herbs. Serve it alongside grilled chicken, sausages or fish, a tender green salad and crisp hot baguettes. Bon appétit! Serves 4-6.

2 lbs.	tiny new potatoes	1 kg
1/2 cup	olive oil	125 mL
2	cloves garlic, minced	2
1/2 cup	minced shallots	125 mL
4	anchovy fillets, finely minced	4
2 tsp.	sugar	10 mL
1/4 cup	white wine vinegar	50 mL
1/3 cup	minced fresh herbs (tarragon, thyme, basil, parsley or any combination)	75 mL
	salt and freshly ground black pepper to taste	
1/3 cup	tiny cured Niçoise-style olives	75 mL

Cut the potatoes in quarters, and cook in gently boiling salted water until just tender when pierced with the tip of a knife. Drain at once, and place in a deep crockery bowl.

While the potatoes are cooking, quickly heat the olive oil and garlic in a skillet until the garlic turns palest golden. Add the shallots and sauté 4-5 minutes, stirring, until softened. Add the anchovies, and sauté 2-3 minutes until the anchovies are "melted" into the sauce. Add the sugar and vinegar, and heat through 1 minute. Remove from heat, and cool to warm.

Pour the mixture over the warm potatoes, and toss very gently to coat. Add the minced fresh herbs and toss. Season with salt and pepper to taste, and toss in the olives.

Set the salad aside in a cool spot (not the refrigerator) for 1 hour to allow the flavours to blend. Toss before serving, and serve cool or at room temperature.

Opposite: (Clockwise from top) Mandarin-Nut Salad (page 124), Pasta and Summer Peppers Salad (page 91), Zorba the Greek Salad (page 94), Sweet Corn and Pepper Salad (page 101).

OTATO PESTO SALAD

Pesto sauce goes with many foods besides pasta. In this quick, economical version of a summer pesto salad, parsley and walnuts are tossed with chunks of potato and crisp snow peas for a side salad that will show off almost any summer meat or fish entrée. Serves 6.

1 1/2 lbs.	unpeeled new or red potatoes, cut into 1 1/2 - 2 inch (4-5 cm) chunks	750 g
4 oz.	snow peas, trimmed	125 g

Parsley-Pesto Sauce:

1 cup	packed fresh parsley sprigs, stems removed	250 mL
1/2 cup	walnut pieces	125 mL
4 tbsp.	grated Parmesan cheese	60 mL
2 tsp.	dried basil	10 mL
2	cloves garlic	2
1/3 cup	olive oil	75 mL

Steam the potatoes for 10 minutes or until just cooked. Allow to cool slightly. Steam the snow peas for 3 minutes, then place in sieve under cold running water to cool. Drain well.

To make the sauce, process the parsley, walnuts, Parmesan, basil and garlic in a blender or food processor until finely chopped. Gradually pour in the oil until well combined.

Place the potatoes and snow peas in a salad bowl and carefully toss with the pesto sauce.

Cover and chill 1 hour before serving.

S UMMER MACARONI AND CHEESE SALAD

This lovely, "stick-to-the-ribs" macaroni and cheese salad makes a great luncheon salad on its own or a wonderful accompaniment to grilled steaks, chops or burgers. It is best prepared several hours before serving, placed in a cool (not cold) spot, and garnished just before serving. Serves 6.

1 lb.	dried pasta (such as shells, ziti, twists, bows, etc.)	500 g
1 tbsp.	*each* salt and olive oil	15 mL
1 cup	*each* sour cream (or yogourt) and mayonnaise, whisked smooth	250 mL
2 tbsp.	whipping cream	30 mL
2-3 tbsp.	prepared horseradish	30-45 mL
1 tsp.	sugar	5 mL
1 tbsp.	dry English-style mustard	15 mL
2 tbsp.	cider vinegar	30 mL
1 tsp.	*each* salt, cracked black peppercorns, dill seed, celery seed	5 mL
4 oz.	*each* finely diced Swiss gruyere and Canadian sharp Cheddar cheese	125 g
2	shallots, finely minced	2
	crisp chilled greens	
3	hard-cooked eggs, chilled, shelled and coarsely chopped	3
2-3 tbsp.	finely minced fresh chives	30-45 mL

Cook the pasta in boiling water with 1 tbsp. (15 mL) each salt and olive oil until al dente (firm to the bite). Drain at once, rinse with cool water, and set aside to cool to room temperature.

Prepare the dressing by whisking together the sour cream and mayonnaise, cream, horseradish, sugar, dry mustard, vinegar, salt, peppercorns, dill and celery seed. Chill the dressing several hours to blend the flavours.

Assemble the salad by gently tossing the room temperature pasta with the dressing. Add the diced cheeses and shallots. Toss well to combine. Let sit in a cool spot 1-2 hours. Mound the salad in a pretty bowl lined with crisp fresh greens. Top the salad with chopped eggs and minced chives and serve.

BROCCOLI AND BACON SALAD

Here is a side salad that looks good and goes well with almost any dish, any occasion. It's colourful, crunchy, and best of all — quick to toss together. Try the dressing with other vegetable combinations too, such as green beans, snow peas and red bell pepper. Serves 4.

Mustard Dressing:

6 tbsp.	vegetable oil	90 mL
2 tbsp.	wine vinegar	30 mL
2 tsp.	Dijon mustard	10 mL
2 tbsp.	chopped fresh parsley	30 mL
	salt and pepper to taste	

Salad:

4 cups	sliced broccoli florets and stems (about 8 oz. (250 g))	1 L
2 cups	quartered mushrooms (about 6 oz. (180 g))	500 mL
12	cherry tomatoes, stemmed and halved	12
6	slices bacon, chopped and cooked	6
4 tbsp.	toasted, sliced almonds	60 mL

To make the dressing, beat the oil, vinegar and mustard in a small bowl until well mixed. Stir in the parsley, salt and pepper.

To make the salad, lightly steam the broccoli about 5 minutes, so it is still crisp. Immediately place it in a sieve and run cold water over it to cool. Drain well. In a serving bowl, toss the broccoli with the mushrooms and tomatoes. Pour on the dressing and toss. Sprinkle the bacon and almonds over the top and serve.

SCALLOP MUSHROOM SALAD

Make this salad early in the day, so that the scallops can "cook" to tender perfection in the delicately flavoured dressing. Serve it alongside Super Simple Grilled Chicken (p. 41) and grilled vegetables. Serves 4.

4 oz.	fresh large scallops	125 g
4 oz.	fresh mushrooms	125 g
2	green onions, finely chopped	2
3 tbsp.	lemon juice	45 mL
2 tbsp.	dry white wine or vinegar	30 mL
1 tbsp.	Dijon mustard	15 mL
1	clove garlic, chopped	1
1/2 cup	olive oil	125 mL
	leaves of butter lettuce for garnish	
	chopped parsley for garnish	

Pat the scallops dry with paper towels, then slice them 1/2 inch (1 cm) thick. Place them in a zip-lock or other sealable plastic bag and add the mushrooms and onions.

In a medium bowl, mix together the lemon juice, wine, mustard and garlic. Slowly add the oil, whisking constantly to make a smooth vinaigrette. Pour the dressing over the scallop mixture and seal the bag. Refrigerate for 4-6 hours, turning the bag occasionally to stir.

At serving time, place the butter lettuce leaves on serving plates and spoon over the scallop mixture. Garnish with the chopped parsley.

TANGY MARINATED SHRIMP

An eye-catching mixture of chilled shrimp served on a bright green bed of lettuce is a wonderful start to a summer dinner party. Make this dish the night before, ready to serve as a starter before Hickory-Smoked Chicken Quarters (p. 42). Top off the dinner with a refreshing Watermelon Slush (p. 149). Serves 6 as a first course, 4 for lunch.

1 cup	vegetable oil	250 mL
1/3 cup	ketchup	75 mL
1/3 cup	vinegar	75 mL
2 tbsp.	Worcestershire sauce	30 mL
2 tsp.	sugar	10 mL
1 tsp.	salt	5 mL
1/2 tsp.	dry mustard	2 mL
dash	bottled hot pepper sauce	dash
1 lb.	hand-peeled cooked fresh shrimp	500 g
1	medium onion, thinly sliced	1
2	bay leaves, crushed	2
	butter lettuce leaves for garnish	

Combine the oil, ketchup, vinegar, Worcestershire sauce, sugar, salt, mustard and hot pepper sauce in a medium bowl and beat until well blended.

In a glass serving bowl, alternate layers of shrimp, onion and crushed bay leaves. Pour the dressing over all. Cover tightly with plastic wrap and chill at least 12 hours before serving.

At serving time, place butter lettuce cups on individual salad plates and spoon the shrimp mixture over top.

INSALATA CAPRESE

This gorgeous salad, vivid with the colours of the Italian flag — bright red tomatoes, creamy white mozzarella cheese, and vibrant green pesto dressing — is a summer show stopper. Serve it with grilled chicken and Italian sausages, hot corn-on-the-cob, and tiny roasted potatoes. Show it off on a rustic crockery or glass platter. Serves 6.

	Fresh Basil Pesto Dressing (recipe follows)	
6	large beefsteak tomatoes	6
3/4 pound	mozzarella cheese, thinly sliced	375 g
1/2 cup	pine nuts, toasted in a 325°F (160°C) oven 8 minutes until golden	125 mL
	salt and cracked black pepper to taste	
	basil for garnish	

Prepare the Fresh Basil Pesto Dressing several hours ahead of time for the best flavour. If chilled, bring to room temperature 30 minutes before using to liquefy (the dressing will turn solid if chilled). To assemble the salad, arrange in concentric circles alternating slices of tomato and mozzarella cheese. Drizzle dressing over the salad down the centre of the rounds. Sprinkle with toasted pine nuts, add salt and pepper, and garnish with sprigs of fresh basil if desired. Serve cool or at room temperature.

FRESH BASIL PESTO DRESSING

2	cloves garlic, minced	2
1 tsp.	salt	5 mL
1 cup	*each* fresh basil leaves (lightly packed) and fresh parsley (stems removed, lightly packed)	250 mL
1/3 cup	freshly grated Parmesan cheese	75 mL
1 cup	olive oil	250 mL
4 tbsp.	balsamic vinegar or red wine vinegar	60 mL

In a food processor fitted with a steel blade, process the garlic and salt to a fine paste, scraping down the sides with a rubber scraper. Add the basil and parsley, and continue to process to a fine mince. Add the Parmesan cheese, and combine. With the motor running, add the olive oil in a thin, steady stream. Finally, add the vinegar. Transfer the dressing to a glass container, cover, and let stand several hours before serving. Whisk the dressing smooth before using.

CLASSIC VINAIGRETTE

A great green salad is only as good as the freshness of the greens — and the dressing! An abundant selection of excellent bottled dressings means you can serve salad any time, but when you want to take a few extra minutes, try this home-made vinaigrette. Add your own favourite herbs and spices for the personal touch. Makes 3/4 cup (175 mL).

1/2 tsp.	salt	2 mL
1	small clove garlic, crushed (optional)	1
2 tsp.	Dijon-style mustard	10 mL
3 tbsp.	red or white wine vinegar	45 mL
pinch	sugar	pinch
1/2 cup	olive oil	125 mL
1 tbsp.	finely minced fresh parsley	15 mL
	freshly ground black pepper to taste	

In a bowl, blender or food processor, combine the salt and garlic. Add the mustard, vinegar and sugar. Whisk in the olive oil, and add the parsley and pepper. The finished vinaigrette should be slightly creamy and very smooth. Use at once, or store tightly capped in the refrigerator for up to 5 days. Shake or whisk smooth before using.

PERSIAN CUCUMBER SALAD

Cool and refreshing, this simple but exotic salad from the Mediterranean is a great starter for a dinner of barbecued ribs and baked potatoes. Serves 4.

1	long English cucumber	1
	salt to taste	
1 cup	yogourt	250 mL
2 tbsp.	white raisins, soaked in 2 tbsp. (30 mL) water	30 mL
2 tbsp.	chopped walnuts	30 mL
1	small onion, minced	1
1/4 tsp.	white pepper	1 mL
1 tbsp.	chopped fresh mint	15 mL
pinch	dried basil	pinch
	lettuce for garnish	

Peel 4 strips of skin from the cucumber, leaving the rest of the skin on for colour, and slice in thin rounds. Place the rounds on a flat plate and salt lightly. Let stand for 30 minutes. Drain off the liquid and pat the cucumber dry. Mix the cucumber with the yogourt. Combine the remaining ingredients and stir into the cucumber mixture. Chill. Serve each portion of salad on a leaf of lettuce.

KIWI CHICKEN SALAD

Here is an unusual, colourful salad to serve for lunch or dinner. Accompanied by fresh crusty bread and butter, it is the ultimate in summer eating, guaranteed to become a favourite with all ages. Serves 4-6.

1	whole chicken breast	1
2 tbsp.	slivered almonds	30 mL
1 tbsp.	butter	15 mL
1/4 tsp.	salt	1 mL
1	10 oz. (284 mL) can mandarin orange segments, drained	1
1/2 cup	fresh or canned pineapple, cut into 1/2 inch (1 cm) cubes	125 mL
2	kiwi fruits, peeled and sliced	2

Dressing:

1/4 tsp.	salt	1 mL
dash	white pepper	dash
1/2 cup	mayonnaise	125 mL
4 tbsp.	yogourt	60 mL
	lettuce leaves for garnish	

Place the chicken breast skin side up on a microproof plate. Cover with waxed paper and microwave on MEDIUM HIGH 70% power 7-9 minutes. Allow it to stand, covered, until slightly cooled.

Bone the chicken. Let it cool and cut the meat into 1/2 inch (1 cm) dice.

Place the slivered almonds, butter and 1/4 tsp. (1 mL) of the salt in a small microproof dish. Microwave on HIGH 100% power in 1 minute increments until the almonds are a light golden brown. Stir after each 1 minute of cooking time. Drain the almonds and spread them on a piece of paper towel to cool.

Make the dressing by blending together all dressing ingredients. Gently toss together the chicken, fruit and dressing. To serve, pile the salad on lettuce leaves and sprinkle with toasted almonds.

TENDER-CRISP VEGETABLE SALAD

A seemingly endless selection of summer vegetable combinations makes the presentation of this salad colourful and innovative. Cook the vegetables until they are just tender-crisp — remember to allow for the continued cooking that takes place during the standing time. Serves 4-6.

10	baby carrots	10
1/2 lb.	green beans	250 g
2	zucchini	2
4	stalks celery	4
1	red bell pepper	1
1	green bell pepper	1

Mayonnaise:

1	egg yolk	1
1 tsp.	dry mustard	5 mL
1/4 tsp.	salt	1 mL
dash	cayenne pepper	dash
2 tbsp.	tarragon vinegar	30 mL
3/4 cup	salad oil	175 mL
1/2 cup	olive oil	125 mL

Wash and trim the vegetables, cutting them into pieces of equal size and length. Cook each vegetable separately in a microproof dish, covered, at HIGH 100% power until just tender-crisp. Stir each vegetable halfway through the cooking time. Allow to cool, cover and chill.

To make the mayonnaise, blend the egg, mustard, salt and cayenne pepper in a blender or food processor. Blend in the vinegar. Very slowly, add the oils to make a thick emulsion. Cover and chill.

To serve, arrange the vegetables attractively on a platter. Pour the mayonnaise over the vegetables, or serve it separately.

QUICK SPINACH SALAD

Here is the traditional spinach salad, only faster and easier because it's all done in the microwave. Everything is prepared ahead, ready for last-minute assembly at serving time — what could be more convenient? Serve the salad as an appetizer, or accompany it with a fresh baguette, butter and a selection of cheeses for a perfect entrée on those hot days of summer. Serves 4-6.

8	slices bacon	8
3	eggs	3
1 1/2 lbs.	fresh spinach	750 g

Dressing:

4 tbsp.	bacon fat	60 mL
2 tbsp.	brown sugar	30 mL
1/2 tsp.	salt	2 mL
1/4 tsp.	white pepper	1 mL
6 tbsp.	white wine vinegar	90 mL
4 tbsp.	finely chopped onion	60 mL
4 tbsp.	toasted pine nuts for garnish	60 mL

Place the bacon on a microproof roasting rack and cover with a piece of paper towel. Microwave on HIGH 100% power 8-10 minutes until the bacon is crisp, rearranging it twice during the cooking time. Allow the bacon to cool and then crumble. Drain off the fat, reserving 4 tbsp. (60 mL) in a 2 cup (500 mL) microproof measure.

Break the eggs onto a microproof plate. Break the yolks and cover with waxed paper. Microwave on MEDIUM 50% power until the eggs are hard-cooked, approximately 4-5 minutes. Allow the eggs to cool and then chop.

Pull and wash the spinach leaves. Layer them in a salad bowl between layers of paper towel and refrigerate until chilled.

Add the remaining dressing ingredients to the reserved bacon fat. Microwave the dressing ingredients on HIGH 100% power 2-3 minutes until the dressing comes to a boil. Remove the paper towel from the chilled spinach, add the bacon and egg and pour on the boiling dressing. Mix thoroughly and serve immediately, topped with toasted pine nuts.

ASPARAGUS WITH TOMATO VINAIGRETTE

The brilliant green of microwave-cooked asparagus, topped with the gorgeous red of the Tomato Vinaigrette, makes this a dish that looks as good as it tastes. It is an ideal accompaniment to poultry or fish, and all by itself it is a delightful light appetizer. Serves 4-6.

2 tbsp.	very finely chopped onion	30 mL
1 - 1 1/2 lbs.	fresh asparagus	500-750 g

Vinaigrette:

3 lbs.	fresh tomatoes	1.5 kg
4 tbsp.	olive oil	60 mL
2 tbsp.	champagne vinegar	30 mL
2 tbsp.	chopped cilantro	30 mL
1 tbsp.	chopped fresh tarragon	15 mL
1/4 tsp.	salt	1 mL
dash	white pepper	dash
	lemon for garnish	

Place the chopped onion in an oblong microproof dish, cover and microwave on HIGH 100% power for 40 seconds.

Trim the asparagus to equal lengths. Divide equally over the onion, placing stalks at both ends of the dish and overlapping tips in the centre. Cover and microwave on HIGH 100% power 8-12 minutes until the asparagus is tender-crisp. Rearrange the asparagus halfway through the cooking time, pulling the stalks from the centre to the outside of the dish. Arrange the asparagus and onion on a serving platter. Cool, then cover and chill.

To make the vinaigrette, cut the tomatoes in half and place them in a microproof dish. Cover and microwave on HIGH 100% power 3-5 minutes until cooked. Push the tomatoes through a sieve to remove the seeds and skin. Return to the dish and microwave, uncovered, on HIGH 100% power until the mixture has been reduced by about half, stirring several times during the cooking. Allow to cool slightly and then mix in the remaining vinaigrette ingredients. Chill. At serving time, spoon the tomato vinaigrette over the asparagus and garnish with lemon.

CHILLED VEGETABLE-PEACH SALAD

One of the great things about summer is the huge, colourful array of choice fresh fruit and vegetables in the produce department. For this recipe choose firm, fresh, juicy peaches for an unusual flavour combination that sets off any grilled meat to luscious perfection. Serves 6.

1/2 cup	diced, peeled new potatoes	125 mL
1/2 cup	slivered baby carrots	125 mL
1/2 cup	halved and slivered green beans	125 mL
1/3 cup	green peas	75 mL
2	large firm peaches	2
2 tsp.	lemon juice	10 mL

Dressing:

1/2 cup	mayonnaise	125 mL
1 1/2 tbsp.	sour cream	20 mL
2 tsp.	Dijon mustard	10 mL
2	green onions, finely chopped	2
1 tbsp.	chopped fresh parsley	15 mL
	freshly ground black pepper to taste	

Cook each vegetable separately in a generous amount of boiling water until just tender-crisp. Run under cold water to stop the cooking, drain and set aside. Plunge the peaches into boiling water for a few seconds, then cool them quickly in cold water. Strip off the skins, slice, then cut the peaches into 1/2 inch (1 cm) cubes. Toss with lemon juice to prevent discolouration. Combine the vegetables and peaches in a large serving bowl.

Combine the dressing ingredients thoroughly and pour half of it over the salad. Toss and chill for up to 2 hours before serving. Taste and adjust the seasonings to taste, adding more pepper if necessary. Serve with any extra dressing on the side.

RAINBOW SALAD

This is one of those side salads that looks as good as it tastes, with the rich colours of papaya, avocado and blueberries. The unusual flavour combination is particularly complementary with fish and chicken dishes. To choose the avocados, check for ripeness: they should give to gentle pressure. Serves 4.

Poppy Seed Dressing:

5 tbsp.	olive oil	75 mL
2 tbsp.	fresh lime juice	30 mL
2 tsp.	honey	10 mL
1 tbsp.	poppy seeds	15 mL

Salad:

1	papaya, halved, seeded, peeled and sliced	1
2	avocados, halved, pitted, peeled and sliced	2
1 cup	blueberries, fresh or frozen (thawed)	250 mL

To make the dressing, beat the olive oil and lime juice in a small bowl until well mixed. Beat in the honey and stir in the poppy seeds.

On 4 salad plates, arrange the papaya and avocado slices beside each other in overlapping lines. Scatter the blueberries down the centre of the papaya slices. Pour the dressing over the salads and serve.

CITRUS FRUIT DIP

A cooling, change-of-pace appetizer, this citrus-flavoured dip is wonderful with apples, pears, grapes, strawberries, bananas, pineapple, kiwi fruit, star fruit, nectarines and plums. Arrange the fruit in colourful groups on a platter or in a country wicker basket accompanied by the dip, and bring it out as a starter for spicy Cajun-Style Steak (p. 10) or Creole-Style Red Snapper (p. 69). This recipe doubles well. Makes 3/4 cup (175 mL).

1	beaten egg	1
4 tbsp.	honey	60 mL
4 tbsp.	orange juice	60 mL
2 tbsp.	lemon juice	30 mL
2 tsp.	butter	10 mL
pinch	salt	pinch
4 tbsp.	whipping cream, whipped	60 mL

Combine all the ingredients except the whipping cream in a medium saucepan and cook, stirring constantly, until slightly thickened. Chill. At serving time, fold in the whipped cream.

The Easy Gourmet features a photograph of this recipe on page 125.

Mandarin-Nut Salad

This is a light, refreshing salad perfect for a luncheon with warm whole-grain rolls, or served at dinner between the main course and dessert. Serves 6.

	fresh spinach	
	romaine lettuce	
1 cup	seedless grapes (red or green), halved	250 mL
1/2 cup	mixed toasted slivered almonds	125 mL
	and pecans, or more to taste	
1	10 oz. (284 mL) can mandarin orange	1
	sections, chilled and drained	

Dressing:

1/2 cup	vegetable oil	125 mL
4 tbsp.	white wine vinegar	60 mL
2 tbsp.	sugar	30 mL
pinch	salt	pinch

1	avocado, peeled and sliced	1

Wash enough spinach and romaine leaves to serve 6 people. Place in a plastic bag with a piece of paper towel until ready to serve. Tear up the spinach and romaine and toss with the grapes, nuts and oranges. Place on chilled salad plates and refrigerate until serving time.

Mix the dressing ingredients in a small bottle and shake well. Just before serving, spoon a little of the dressing on each salad and garnish with slices of avocado. Serve any remaining dressing on the side.

The Easy Gourmet features a photograph of this recipe on page 107.

Opposite: (Top to bottom) Vegetable Medley with Creamy Herb Dip (page 87), Gado Gado (page 92), Citrus Fruit Dip (page 123).

SUMMER COMPLEMENTS

In this section, you'll find the special warm weather recipes that inspire an outdoor luncheon or add the perfect touch to a barbecue: soups like chilled Summer Tomato Soup and Green Gazpacho; elegant deli-style sandwiches like Creamy Beef-on-a-Bagel and Mediterranean Deli Sandwiches; cooling beverages like Citrus-Spiced Sun Tea and Watermelon Slush. For dessert, try Glazed Fruit Flan or Summer Berry Ice Cream Pie—guaranteed to complement the taste of summer!

CHILLED CARROT CREAM SOUP

Here is a wonderful excuse to pick up lots of those fresh young carrots so plentiful in the summer. The soup may be served hot, but the subtle creamy flavour is even more pronounced if the soup is chilled. Serves 4-6.

2	leeks, white part only, sliced	2
1	clove garlic, chopped	1
1 tbsp.	butter	15 mL
1 lb.	young carrots	500 g
2	10 oz. (284 mL) cans beef broth	2
1/2 tsp.	salt	2 mL
1/4 tsp.	*each* black pepper and nutmeg	1 mL
1 cup	whipping cream	250 mL
	chopped fresh parsley for garnish	

Place the leeks, garlic, and butter in a microproof dish. Cover and microwave on HIGH 100% power 2-3 minutes until the leek is soft, stirring once during the cooking time. Scrub and trim the carrots and slice in equal size pieces. Add to the leek mixture, cover and microwave on HIGH 100% power 5-8 minutes the until carrot is soft, stirring once during the cooking time.

Blend in the beef broth, cover and microwave on MEDIUM 50% power 15 minutes. Reduce the power level further, if necessary, to prevent the mixture from boiling. Allow to cool slightly and then blend in a food processor until smooth. Add the salt, pepper and nutmeg. Adjust the seasonings to taste. Chill the soup for at least 1 hour.

To serve, swirl the cream into the soup and sprinkle a little chopped parsley on each dish.

C HILLED HARVEST SQUASH SOUP

This delightful summer soup features fresh summer squash — resulting in a beautiful pale orange-hued colour. Serve icy cold in delicate glass bowls, garnishing each serving with a swirl of whipping cream, a thin slice of lemon, and a sprinkling of chives. Add a hearty Black Forest ham and cheese sandwich tucked inside a freshly baked croissant, and a pitcher of mint-laced iced tea. A perfect summer luncheon or supper! Serves 4-6.

3/4 lb.	*each* pattypan and crookneck squashes, trimmed and cut into 1 inch (2.5 cm) pieces, about 1 1/2 lbs. (750 g) total	375 g
2	large russet potatoes, peeled and cut into 1 inch (2.5 cm) chunks	2
1	medium onion, diced	1
2	stalks celery, cut into 1 inch (2.5 cm) pieces	2
3 cups	rich chicken stock	750 mL
1/2 cup	fresh orange juice	125 mL
	grated rind of 1 orange	
1 tbsp.	*each* curry powder, ground ginger, brown sugar	15 mL
1 tsp.	*each* ground coriander and allspice	5 mL
1 cup	whipping cream	250 mL
2 tbsp.	fresh lemon juice	30 mL
	salt and freshly ground pepper to taste	
1/2 cup	whipping cream, chilled (optional)	125 mL
4-6	thin slices lemon or orange	4-6
4 tbsp.	snipped fresh chives	60 mL

In a large stock pot, combine the squashes, potatoes, onion, celery, chicken broth, orange juice, orange rind, curry powder, ginger, sugar, coriander and allspice. Bring the mixture to a gentle boil, partially cover, and cook until the vegetables are very tender, about 35-45 minutes. Remove from the heat, and allow to cool to barely warm, about 20 minutes.

Using a food processor fitted with a steel blade, purée the vegetables in small batches until very smooth. Add the reserved stock to each batch of purée. Return the puréed mixture and all stock to the pot. Bring to a simmer, and cook gently. Whisk in 1 cup (250 mL) cream and simmer the soup over low heat 10-15 minutes. Season with lemon juice, salt and pepper. Taste and correct the seasonings.

Cool the soup. Chill, tightly covered, until ready to serve. Ladle into bowls, and garnish each serving with a swirl of chilled whipping cream, a thin slice of lemon or orange, and a sprinkling of snipped chives.

Note: When fall butternut squash is in season, try this recipe using 1 1/2 lbs. (750 g) trimmed, peeled, cubed squash for a delightful variation.

BLACK FOREST AND CHEESE CROISSANT STACK-UP

Freshly-baked croissants from the deli or in-store bakery are wonderful to keep on hand to split and fill with deli meats and cheeses for elegant, savoury sandwiches. Try this combo of thinly shaved Black Forest ham and cheese with honey mustard, mayonnaise and a handful of fresh sprouts. Serves 4.

4	large croissants	4
	honey mustard	
4 oz.	thinly sliced Edam *or* Gouda cheese	125 g
8 oz.	shaved Black Forest ham	250 g
	mayonnaise	
	alfalfa sprouts	

Warm the croissants in a heated 350°F (180°C) oven on a cookie sheet for 5 minutes until crispy. Remove, cool 7 minutes, and split open using a very sharp serrated knife.

Spread a thin film of honey mustard on the bottom half of each croissant. Fold and layer, alternately, the cheese and ham slices. Spread a thin film of mayonnaise over the final layer. Top with sprouts, and close with the upper halves of the croissants. Secure with wooden sandwich picks, and serve at once.

SUMMER CORN CHOWDER WITH RED PEPPER PURÉE

Make this lovely corn chowder when you have a bushel-basket of fresh summer corn. In a pinch, frozen corn kernels are almost as good! Serve barely warm in colourful crockery bowls, topping each serving with a spoonful of red pepper purée. Add a final confetti-like sprinkling of diced bell peppers, and this hearty soup becomes true party fare. Open-faced sandwiches of deli-style pâté on fresh sourdough bread, topped with honey mustard, thinly sliced cucumber and crisp sprouts are an ideal accompaniment. Serves 4-6.

6	slices bacon, diced	6
1	small onion, peeled and minced	1
1	*each* red and green bell pepper, diced	1
2 cups	diced potato (2 medium potatoes)	500 mL
1 cup	milk	250 mL
1	10 oz. (284 mL) can chicken broth	1
4 cups	whole kernel corn (fresh or frozen)	1 L
1 tsp.	*each* salt, sugar and dried thyme	5 mL
1/2 - 1 cup	whipping cream	125-250 mL
10-12 drops	bottled hot pepper sauce	10-12 drops
	freshly ground black pepper to taste	
	Red Pepper Purée (recipe follows)	
2/3 cup	diced mixed bell peppers for garnish	150 mL

Sauté the bacon in a large stock pot over medium heat until softened and pale golden. Add the onion and diced peppers, and sauté until just tender. Add the potatoes, milk and broth. Partially cover and simmer until the potatoes are tender, about 30 minutes.

Purée 1 cup (250 mL) of the corn and add it to the chowder along with the remaining corn. Add the salt, sugar and thyme and bring the chowder to a simmer. Partially cover and cook 15 minutes, until the soup is bubbly and the corn is tender. Stir in the cream to the desired consistency. Simmer the chowder 10 minutes to heat through, adding hot pepper sauce and pepper and adjust the seasonings to taste.

To serve, ladle warm chowder into bowls, topping each serving with a spoonful of Red Pepper Purée and a sprinkling of diced peppers.

RED PEPPER PURÉE

12 oz.	bottled roasted red peppers, drained	340 mL
1 tbsp.	*each* sugar and sherry vinegar or red wine vinegar	15 mL

In a food processor fitted with a steel blade, purée the red pepper, adding the sugar and vinegar. Store in a glass jar, tightly capped and chilled until ready to use.

COUNTRY-FRENCH PÂTÉ SANDWICHES

Look for pâté in the deli department and keep several kinds on hand to create instant gourmet-style sandwiches. Garnish with pretty slices of cucumber, watercress, thinly sliced cornichons and sprouts. Build each sandwich on fresh crisp croissants or sourdough bread. Makes 6 sandwiches.

6	croissants or 1/2 inch (1 cm) thick slices sourdough bread	6
	honey mustard	
8 oz.	deli-style pâté (try Pepper Pâté or Country Style Pâté)	250 g
1/2	long English cucumber, unpeeled, sliced into paper-thin rounds	1/2
6	sour *or* sweet cornichons, thinly sliced, with stems attached, fanned out	6
	crisp watercress sprigs or sprouts	

Slice the croissants open with a sharp, serrated knife. Spread the croissants or bread with a film of honey mustard. Top each with thin slices of pâté, including some of the shimmering gelée. Garnish with thin slices of cucumber, fanned-out cornichons, and sprigs of crisp watercress or sprouts. Serve at once.

GARDEN PEA BISQUE WITH GARLIC-MINT CROUTONS

This is a lovely, delicately-flavoured chilled pea soup — vibrant green in colour, creamy in consistency, and flecked with fresh herbs. Serve in pretty shallow glass bowls, garnish with dollops of sour cream and crispy garlic-and-mint flavoured croutons. Add a hearty deli sandwich and you have a simple yet elegant summer meal. Serves 4.

4 tbsp.	butter	60 mL
1	medium onion, minced	1
1 tbsp.	sugar	15 mL
3 cups	rich chicken stock	750 mL
1	large russet potato, peeled and diced	1
4 cups	fresh or frozen young peas	1 L
3 tbsp.	*each* minced fresh mint, chervil and parsley	45 mL
1 cup	*each* half-and-half and whipping cream	250 mL
1/2 tsp.	*each* ground nutmeg	2 mL
	and white pepper	
	salt to taste	
1/2 cup	sour cream	125 mL
	Garlic-Mint Croutons (recipe follows)	
	sprigs of fresh mint for garnish	

Heat the butter over medium-high heat until bubbly. Add the onion, and sauté until tender and pale golden. Add the sugar and sauté 2 minutes to caramelize slightly. Add the chicken stock and potato and bring to a simmer. Partially cover the pot and cook until the potato is very tender, about 15 minutes. Add the peas and simmer 7-8 minutes (if using frozen peas, defrost first). Stir in the mint, chervil, parsley and heat 1 minute.

Cool the mixture to barely warm. In small batches, purée the mixture in a food processor fitted with a steel blade. Transfer puréed mixture to stock pot, add the half-and-half, whipping cream, nutmeg, white pepper and salt to taste. Heat gently over low heat 5-7 minutes, stirring, to heat through. Cool soup, cover and chill until ready to serve.

Ladle the soup into shallow bowls, garnish each with a generous dollop of sour cream, a sprinkling of croutons and a sprig of fresh mint.

GARLIC-MINT CROUTONS

3 tbsp.	*each* butter and olive oil	45 mL
1	large clove garlic, crushed	1
1 1/2 cups	crustless day-old bread,	375 mL
	cut into 1/4 inch (5 mm) dice	
2 tbsp.	dried mint leaves, crushed	30 mL
	salt and freshly ground black pepper to taste	

In a large skillet, heat the butter and oil until bubbly over medium heat. Add the garlic and sauté, stirring, 1 minute. Toss in the cubed bread, stirring quickly to coat, and sauté the croutons 5-6 minutes until pale golden brown and crispy on all sides. Remove skillet from heat. Season at once, while hot, with crumbed mint, and a light sprinkling of salt and pepper to taste. Pour the hot croutons out onto a paper bag to cool, and serve within several hours of preparation.

C HICKEN SALAD ON DILLED RYE

Stop at the deli department, pick up a container of freshly prepared chicken salad, a loaf of dilled rye bread, some thinly sliced Canadian Swiss cheese — and you've got the makings of a great sandwich. Serves 4.

1	loaf dilled rye bread	1
3/4 lb.	prepared chicken salad	375 g
8 oz.	thinly sliced Canadian Swiss cheese	250 g
	mayonnaise	
1-2	firm ripe tomatoes, thinly sliced	1-2
	Dijon mustard (optional)	
	sprouts	

Spread 4 slices bread with the chicken salad. Add the gently folded slices of Swiss cheese. Add mayonnaise, and several thin slices of tomato. Spread each top piece of bread with mustard, if desired. Tuck in a generous handful of fresh sprouts. Top with bread, cut in half, secure the sandwich with wooden picks, and serve.

CHILLED MINESTRONE WITH PESTO

Minestrone, that standby of Italian soups, is traditionally served hot as a prelude to a hearty Italian meal. This version is for summer — chilled, loaded with summer vegetables, and enlivened with a zesty pesto sauce. Serve it with a bowl of freshly grated Parmesan, home-made oversize bread sticks, and a platter of assorted cheeses and grapes for dessert. Serve it all up on the patio, and think of Italy! Serves 6-8.

1/3 cup	olive oil	75 mL
1	medium onion, diced	1
2	leeks, sliced into rounds	2
3	red potatoes, cut into 1/2 inch (1 cm) cubes	3
2	zucchini, halved lengthwise and cut into 1/2 inch (1 cm) thick half-rounds	2
4	crookneck squash, cut into 1/2 inch (1 cm) dice	4
1/2 lb.	fresh green beans, cut diagonally into 2 inch (5 cm) lengths	250 g
1/2 lb.	peas, shelled	250 g
2	large carrots, halved lengthwise and cut into 1/2 inch (1 cm) rounds	2
1 lb.	Swiss chard, cut crosswise into 1/2 inch (1 cm) wide "ribbons"	500 g
5	tomatoes, seeded and coarsely diced	5
6 cups	de-fatted chicken stock or water	1.5 L
1 tsp.	*each* dried thyme, salt, cracked black pepper, sugar	5 mL
1	bay leaf	1
1 cup	frozen lima beans	250 mL
3/4 cup	small pasta (shells, bows, etc.)	175 mL
	Fresh Basil Pesto (recipe follows)	
1 cup	freshly grated Parmesan cheese	250 mL

Heat the olive oil in a large stock pot over medium-high heat. Add the onion and leeks, and sauté over medium heat until the vegetables are softened. Add the potatoes, zucchini, squash, green beans, peas, carrots, chard and tomatoes, and sauté 5 minutes. Add the stock and bring to a simmer. Stir in the thyme, salt, pepper, sugar and bay leaf. Partially cover the soup and cook over medium-low heat 35-40 minutes, or until the vegetables are tender. Add the lima beans and pasta, and cook 25 minutes more until the pasta is al dente (do not overcook). Taste the soup and correct for seasonings. Remove from heat and cool. Chill until ready to serve, at least 8 hours.

To serve, ladle cool (not ice-cold) soup into deep crockery soup bowls. Add a generous spoonful of Fresh Basil Pesto to each serving, stirring in to flavour the soup. Pass Parmesan to sprinkle over each serving.

FRESH BASIL PESTO

1 tsp.	salt	5 mL
2	cloves garlic, minced	2
2 cups	fresh basil leaves, packed	500 mL
1/2 cup	fresh parsley sprigs, packed	125 mL
1 tbsp.	grated lemon rind	15 mL
3/4 cup	freshly grated Parmesan cheese	175 mL
3/4 cup	olive oil	175 mL

In a food processor fitted with a steel blade, process the salt and garlic to a fine paste, scraping down the sides. Add the basil and parsley, and process to a very fine purée. Add the lemon rind and Parmesan, and process 15 seconds. With the motor running, add the olive oil in a slow, thin, steady stream. Transfer the pesto to a glass jar, cap tightly, and chill until ready to use. Bring to room temperature before using.

Note: This soup is also delicious served warm.

SUMMER TOMATO SOUP

This delightful fresh tomato soup is like no other — redolent with the flavour of fresh tomatoes, perfumed with good olive oil, fresh basil and a hint of garlic. Serve hot, warm or chilled, accompanied by the hot Crostini, or a sandwich of split deli-style bagels filled with Winnipeg cream cheese, shaved beef and slivered red onion. Serves 4-6.

3 lbs.	fresh ripe tomatoes	1.5 kg
1/2 cup	olive oil	125 mL
2	large cloves garlic, crushed	2
2 tsp.	sugar	10 mL
1/4 cup	minced fresh basil	50 mL
2 tbsp.	minced fresh parsley	30 mL
3 cups	rich beef stock	750 mL
	salt and freshly ground black pepper to taste	
	sprigs of fresh basil for garnish	
	Hot Crostini (recipe follows)	

Plunge the tomatoes into boiling water for 20 seconds and slip the skins off. Seed the tomatoes and chop coarsely. In a large stock pot, heat the olive oil over medium heat and add the tomatoes. "Sweat" the tomatoes in the hot oil, mashing with the back of a spoon if needed, until pulpy and softened. Cook uncovered 10-12 minutes. Add the garlic, sugar, basil and parsley, and cook 2-3 minutes. Add the beef stock and bring the soup just to a simmer. Simmer 5-7 minutes to heat through. Season to taste with salt and pepper. Remove from heat.

Ladle into wide, shallow bowls and top each serving with a sprig of fresh basil. Serve with toasted Crostini.

CROSTINI

8-12	1/2 inch (1 cm) thick slices baguette, cut on the diagonal	8-12
	olive oil	
1/2 cup	grated Parmesan cheese	125 mL

Brush the bread slices generously with olive oil. Place on a cookie sheet, and sprinkle the tops generously with Parmesan. Bake in a 350°F (180°C) oven 10 minutes until toasted and golden brown on top. Serve hot.

CREAMY BEEF-ON-A-BAGEL SANDWICH

The deli department or in-store bakery offers wonderful bagels in a myriad of flavours. Keep a bag on hand for quick-as-a-flash sandwiches on a moment's notice. Heat the bagels in a 350°F (180°C) for 5 minutes before splitting and filling. This combo features Winnipeg cream cheese, zesty peppered eye-of-round beef, and onion slivers. Makes 4-6 sandwiches.

4-6	deli-style bagels (plain, poppyseed or sesame seed)	4-6
4 oz.	Winnipeg cream cheese	125 g
8 oz.	thinly sliced peppered eye-of-round beef	250 g
1	red onion, peeled and sliced into paper-thin rounds	1
1/3 cup	prepared horseradish (optional)	75 mL
	leaf lettuce	

Warm the bagels if necessary. Split them open using a very sharp, serrated knife. Whip the cream cheese smooth, and spread over the bottom halves of the bagels. Top with thin slices of beef, gently folding and layering. Top with thin slices of red onion. Add a thin layer of prepared horseradish if desired. Tuck in leaf lettuce, top with the bagel lids, secure with wooden picks and serve.

C HICKEN WATERCRESS CHOWDER

This is a delicately flavoured soup that may be served warm or chilled as a delightful light summer luncheon. Accompany it with melba toast or toasted bread sticks, followed by a light salad and fruit for dessert. Serves 4-6.

6-8 oz.	chicken pieces	180-250 g
1	medium onion, chopped	1
1	small clove garlic, chopped	1
1	medium potato, peeled and chopped	1
2 tbsp.	butter	30 mL
1/4 tsp.	ground mace	1 mL
1	bay leaf	1
2	bunches watercress	2
2	10 oz. (284 mL) cans chicken broth	2
	salt and white pepper to taste	
4 tbsp.	whipping cream	60 mL

Remove the skin from the chicken. Place it on a microproof plate, with the thicker portions towards the outside edge of the dish. Cover with waxed paper and microwave on MEDIUM HIGH 70% power 8-10 minutes until cooked. Cool slightly, remove the meat from the bone and chop the meat.

Place the onion, garlic, potato and butter in a microproof casserole dish. Cover and microwave on HIGH 100% power 4-6 minutes until the vegetables are soft, stirring at least once during the cooking time. Stir in the ground mace and bay leaf.

Wash the watercress and reserve a few sprigs for garnish. Add the watercress and chicken broth to the vegetables in the casserole dish. Cover and microwave on HIGH 100% power 10-15 minutes to bring to a boil. Reduce the power level to MEDIUM 50% power and allow to simmer 30 minutes, reducing the power level further, if necessary, to prevent boiling.

Allow to cool, discard the bay leaf, add the chopped chicken meat and liquidize in a blender or food processor. Add salt and white pepper to taste. Blend in the cream, cover and chill.

Serve garnished with reserved sprigs of watercress.

GREEN GAZPACHO

Try this lovely, cool green version of the more traditional red gazpacho, redolent with cucumber, green pepper, celery and green onions. Serve it in glass bowls, icy cold, with a garnish of sour cream and sliced green onions. A spoonful of toasted almonds is a wonderful — and surprising — addition. Serves 6.

2 tsp.	salt	10 mL
2	cloves garlic, minced	2
3	long English cucumbers, washed and cut into chunks	3
1	bunch green onions, trimmed and washed	1
2	green bell peppers, seeded and cut into chunks	2
6	stalks celery, leaves trimmed, cut into pieces	6
6	green tomatoes, cut into chunks	6
1 cup	ice water	250 mL
2 cups	sour cream or yogourt	500 mL
3 tbsp.	*each* olive oil and white wine vinegar	45 mL
	freshly ground black pepper to taste	
	sour cream for garnish	
1 cup	sliced green onions (optional) for garnish	250 mL
1 cup	slivered almonds, toasted in a 325°F (160°C) oven 8-10 minutes until rich golden brown	250 mL

In a food processor fitted with a steel blade, process the salt and garlic to a fine paste, scraping down sides. Add, a small batch at a time, the cucumbers, green onion, green pepper, celery and green tomatoes and process to a chunky, medium-coarse puree. Transfer the pureed soup to a large crockery bowl. Whisk in the ice water, sour cream, olive oil and vinegar. Add liberal grindings of black pepper. Cover the soup and chill several hours, or overnight for even better flavour.

To serve, ladle the iced soup into chilled bowls (or into bowls set over crushed ice). Top each serving with a dollop of chilled sour cream, a spoonful of sliced green onions, and a spoonful of toasted almonds. Serve at once.

RED GAZPACHO

Gazpacho never seems to go out of culinary fashion. Chock full of ripe tomatoes, cucumbers, peppers, onion and seasonings, this soup is wonderful served icy cold in chilled bowls. Add a deli sandwich and you have a complete summer meal. Serves 6-8.

1 1/2 cups	cubed French bread, crusts removed	375 mL
1/3 cup	*each* olive oil and red wine vinegar	75 mL
1/2 tsp.	sugar	2 mL
12 drops	bottled hot pepper sauce	12 drops
1 tsp.	salt	5 mL
2	cloves garlic, slivered	2
2	large cucumbers, peeled and cut into chunks	2
8	large tomatoes, seeded and coarsely chopped	8
1	*each* red and green bell pepper	1
1	medium onion, cut into chunks	1
2 cups	tomato or V-8 juice, chilled	500 mL
1 cup	beef broth or bouillon, chilled and de-fatted	250 mL
1 tbsp.	Worcestershire sauce	15 mL
	freshly ground black pepper to taste	
2 cups	Spanish Croutons (recipe follows)	500 mL
1 cup	*each* diced green pepper, diced cucumber, diced red pepper, and sliced green onion	250 mL

Toast the bread cubes on a cookie sheet in a 300°F (150°C) oven 10 minutes, until pale golden. Remove, place in a crockery bowl and add the olive oil, vinegar, sugar and hot pepper sauce. Set aside for 1-2 hours.

In a food processor fitted with a steel blade, process the salt and garlic to a fine paste. Add the cucumbers, tomatoes, peppers and onion and process, in several batches, to coarse purée. Process the entire bread mixture along with the final batch to a purée. Return the soup mixture to the bowl. Whisk in the tomato juice, beef stock and Worcestershire sauce. Add liberal grindings of black pepper. Taste and correct for seasonings. Chill the soup 8 hours or overnight. Serve it icy cold, ladled into chilled bowls. Pass the croutons and diced vegetables.

SPANISH CROUTONS

1/3 cup	olive oil	75 mL
1	small clove garlic, crushed	1
2 cups	diced home-style white or	500 mL
	French bread, crusts removed	
	paprika and salt to taste	

Heat the olive oil in a large non-stick skillet over medium heat. Add the garlic, swirl it around for 2 minutes, and discard. Add the bread cubes, toss quickly to coat, and fry until golden brown and crispy. Turn the croutons out onto a paper bag and season with a very light sprinkling of paprika and salt. Cool to room temperature. Serve within 2-3 hours of preparation.

The Easy Gourmet features a photograph of this recipe on page 143.

MEDITERRANEAN DELI SANDWICH

The deli department makes sandwiches a snap! Try this Mediterranean-inspired sandwich with chilled soup for a perfect, light summer meal. Makes 4 sandwiches.

1	loaf crusty French bread	1
	grainy mustard	
4 oz.	*each* very thinly sliced Black Forest ham, turkey	125 g
	breast, herbed salami and prosciutto	
8 oz.	very thinly sliced mozzarella cheese	250 g
2	*each* marinated whole red and yellow peppers	2
	or substitute 1/4 lb. (125 g) prepared antipasto	

Cut the bread into four 6 inch (15 cm) pieces. Cut lengthwise.

Spread the bottom halves of bread with grainy mustard. Gently fold and layer thinly sliced ham, turkey breast, salami, and prosciutto alternately with sliced cheese. Slice the peppers lengthwise into quarters, seed and pat dry. Add 1 slice *each* red and yellow pepper to each sandwich. Top each with a bread lid, fasten the sandwiches together with wooden picks, and serve.

The Easy Gourmet features a photograph of this recipe on page 143.

N ON-ALCOHOLIC SUMMER SANGRIA

Try this alcohol-free version of the classic Spanish fruit-laden wine cooler. Serve it over ice in your prettiest tall glass pitcher, garnishing each serving with a bit of the fruit. Makes about ten 8 oz. (250 mL) glassfuls.

1	40 oz. (1.14 L) bottle cranberry cocktail, chilled	1
1/2 cup	fresh orange juice	125 mL
	juice of 1 lemon	
	juice of 1 lime	
1	*each* whole orange, lemon and lime sliced into thin rounds	1
1 cup	fresh strawberries, halved	250 mL
2	fresh peaches, thinly sliced	2
1	small apple, cut into thin wedges	1
2 tbsp.	sugar	30 mL
1	26 oz. (750 mL) bottle club soda, chilled	1
	ice cubes	
	fresh whole berries and peach slices for garnish	

Combine the cranberry cocktail, orange juice, lemon juice, lime juice, sliced citrus fruits, strawberries, peaches and apple with the sugar. Stir to dissolve the sugar and refrigerate the mixture 2-3 hours. Before serving, add the chilled soda. Serve over ice, with each glass decorated with fresh fruit.

The Easy Gourmet features a photograph of this recipe on page 89.

Opposite: (Top to bottom) Double B.C. Berry Shortcake (page 151), Cranapple Fizz (page 147), Mediterranean Deli Sandwich (page 141), Red Gazpacho (page 140).

CY SUMMER LATTE

Latte is a wildly popular Italian version of morning coffee — hot steamed milk with an infusion of strong espresso and a foamy head, equally delicious iced in the summer and served in tall cooler glasses. Make it up in a big pitcher, and serve at a summer brunch for a delightful twist on the more familiar mug-o! Makes four 8 oz. (250 mL) cupfuls.

4-5 tbsp.	instant espresso crystals	60-75 mL
1 cup	boiling water	250 mL
3 1/2 cups	milk	875 mL
2 tbsp.	sugar	30 mL
	crushed ice or	
	cracked ice cubes	
	cinnamon or cocoa	
	long cinnamon sticks	
	(optional) for stirring	

Dissolve the espresso in boiling water and set aside. Pour the milk into a deep saucepan, and heat gently to just below a simmer (do not allow the milk to boil). Whisk the milk constantly as it heats, whipping during the final 2-3 minutes to create a foamy consistency. Remove the milk from the heat, and add the sugar and dissolved espresso. Whisk to combine. Set aside to cool to room temperature.

Fill 4 tall cooler glasses with crushed ice. Whisk the cooled latte until frothy. Fill the glasses, whisking the final bit of liquid to a great, foamy texture. Spoon foam on top of each cupful, and sprinkle with either cinnamon or cocoa. Add a cinnamon stick for stirring if desired.

Note: For a more lavish, almost dessert-like beverage, top each portion with softly whipped cream instead of spooning on the last bit of whipped latte. For 4 servings, whip 1/2 cup (125 mL) chilled whipping cream to soft, billowy peaks with 1 tbsp. (15 mL) powdered sugar and several drops pure vanilla extract. Divide this mixture among the iced lattes, and sprinkle with cinnamon or cocoa.

CITRUS-SPICED SUN TEA

If you've never tried making tea with cold tap water, you are in for a treat. The result is a clear, absolutely non-bitter brew, steeped in the sun for an hour or two, or in the refrigerator overnight. No hot stove, no instantly-melting ice cubes, no muss, no fuss! Makes 1 quart (1 L).

1 quart	clear, cold tap water (let the water run 60 seconds before measuring)	1 L
4	tea bags (Darjeeling, English Breakfast and Orange Pekoe are all good choices) *or* 3 tbsp. (45 mL) loose tea leaves in an infuser	4
1	continuous thin spiral orange rind from 1 small orange (no white pith)	1
1	continuous thin spiral lemon rind from 1 small lemon (no white pith)	1
	ice cubes	
	thin slices lemon and orange	
	berry sugar to taste	
	fresh mint leaves	

Combine the water, tea and citrus rinds in a glass jar or pitcher with a lid. Place in the sun for several hours until it turns a rich golden brown, or place in the refrigerator overnight. Remove the citrus rinds and discard.

Serve the tea over cracked ice or ice cubes in tall cooler glasses. Add a thin slice of lemon and orange to each serving. Sweeten to taste with sugar, and tuck in a fresh sprig of mint as garnish.

Note: For a spicier version, add a 2 inch (5 cm) long cinnamon stick, 3-4 whole allspice berries, and 4-5 whole cloves to the tea mixture. Discard after the tea has steeped.

The Easy Gourmet features a photograph of this recipe on the front cover.

O LD-FASHIONED LEMON-LIMEADE

Nothing seems to quench a summer thirst like good old-fashioned lemonade. This version adds a snap of tangy lime to the more familiar lemon. Prepare it with clear, cold tap water or, for a wonderful fizzy version, try it with club soda! Serve in tall, frosty glasses with pretty swizzle sticks and slices of lemon and lime. Makes 4 servings.

2/3 cup	fresh lemon juice	150 mL
1/3 cup	fresh lime juice	75 mL
2/3 - 1 cup	berry sugar to taste	150-250 mL
14	ice cubes	14
4 cups	ice-cold tap water (let it run 60 seconds before measuring) *or* chilled club soda	1 L
	each whole lemon and whole lime, cut into paper-thin slices	

Combine the lemon juice, lime juice and sugar, stir to dissolve the sugar and allow to sit at room temperature 15 minutes. Add the ice cubes, water and citrus slices. Stir to combine thoroughly until the pitcher is completely frosted. Pour into tall cooler glasses, and serve at once, icy cold.

C RANAPPLE FIZZ

Cool, tangy-sweet and full of Vitamin C, this drink was made for summer. Soda adds a gorgeous sparkle. Makes 1 large glassful.

1/2 cup	cranberry juice	125 mL
1/2 cup	clear apple juice	125 mL
	club soda	
	ice cubes	

Mix the juices together in a tall glass. Top up with soda and add ice cubes. Serve immediately.

The Easy Gourmet features a photograph of this recipe on page 143.

PEACH-NECTARINE MILKSHAKE

Cool, creamy and full of the summertime taste of fresh fruit, this shake is a winner with family and friends of any age. You can make it with raspberries (fresh or whole frozen) and raspberry swirl ice cream, strawberries and strawberry ice cream, or any other combination you like. Makes 1 large glassful.

1	medium ripe nectarine	1
4	large scoops peach ice cream	4
4 oz.	cold milk	125 mL
dash	vanilla	dash

Purée the fruit in a blender. Add the ice cream and blend. With the machine running, pour in the milk and vanilla. Serve at once.

BANANA ORANGE FROSTIE

Here is a treat for you and your summer guests to enjoy while you're waiting for the barbecue to heat up. Bananas and oranges were made for each other! Use soft, overripe bananas to get a super-smooth purée. Makes 2 large glassfuls.

1	large ripe banana	1
1 cup	orange sherbet	250 mL
1 cup	orange juice	250 mL
6-8	ice cubes	6-8

Blend the banana with the orange sherbet. Add orange juice until the mixture reaches the consistency you like. Add the ice cubes and blend until coarsely chopped. Serve immediately.

INEAPPLE SMOOTHIE

This poolside treat is made with fresh pineapple — available all year, and especially satisfying in the warm weather. You'll find fresh pineapple in the produce department, peeled, cored, and ready to go. Serves 8.

1	fresh pineapple	1
1 cup	fresh orange juice	250 mL
1 quart	vanilla ice cream	1 L
	club soda	

Core and peel the pineapple. Purée it in a food processor with the orange juice, until very smooth. Slowly spoon in the ice cream, blending until thick and creamy. Fill each glass half full, top up with soda, and stir.

ATERMELON SLUSH

Icy cold watermelon means summer! Whipped up with ice and soda, it's a colourful, sparkling beverage perfect for outdoor living. Children love it. Best of all, it freezes well, so you can put some away for a surprise treat in the winter. Makes 2 large glassfuls.

1/4	large watermelon	1/4
	ice cubes	
	club soda	
	mint sprigs for garnish	

Peel and seed the melon. Purée until smooth in a blender. Add a few ice cubes and purée, repeating until the mixture is a smooth slush. You can freeze it at this point (it thaws quickly and can be chopped up and reblended). To serve, fill each glass 3/4 full of slush and top with a little soda. Garnish with sprigs of mint.

Note: To serve as a sorbet, omit the soda and spoon into small parfait glasses. Garnish with mint and serve.

TRIPLE-BERRY TRIFLE

This spectacular summer trifle takes only 20 minutes to assemble, waits for several days in the refrigerator, and commands raves from all who taste it. Serve — and stand back for compliments! Serves 8-10.

1 lb.	raspberry jam-filled sponge cake jelly roll, sliced 1/4 inch (5 mm) thick	500 g
1/3 cup	cream sherry	75 mL
1	8 oz. (250 mL) jar raspberry jam	1
1	4 oz. (135 g) package vanilla pudding	1
3 1/2 cups	half-and-half cream	875 mL
1 cup	fresh raspberries	250 mL
1 cup	fresh strawberries, sliced	250 mL
2 cups	whipping cream	500 mL
2 tbsp.	icing sugar	30 mL
1 tsp.	pure vanilla extract	5 mL
1/3 cup	toasted slivered or sliced almonds	75 mL
	whole raspberries and sprigs of fresh mint for garnish	

Line the bottom and sides of a shallow glass 3 quart (3 L) bowl with 2/3 of the jelly roll slices, fitting them close together with no spaces in between. Brush generously with some of the sherry. Spread two-thirds of the jam generously over the cake rounds.

Meanwhile, prepare the pudding according to package directions, using the half-and-half cream instead of milk. Ladle 2/3 of the hot pudding over the jam-topped cake. Scatter 2/3 of the berries over the pudding. Top with the reserved cake rounds, brush with the remaining sherry, and top with the remainder of the jam and the remaining berries. Ladle the remaining pudding over top. Seal at once with plastic wrap to prevent a skin from forming. Chill several hours or up to 3 days before serving.

A few hours before serving, whip the whipping cream with the icing sugar and vanilla until soft peaks form. Spread the cream over the top of the trifle right to the edges of the bowl. Cover and chill.

To serve, garnish with almonds, berries and mint. Plunge a serving spoon into the trifle right to the base of the bowl and spoon up generous portions.

DOUBLE B.C. BERRY SHORTCAKE

Nothing says summer like a mile-high berry shortcake! The produce department makes it even better when you combine two varieties of fresh berries, and the in-store bakery makes it simple with the marvelous "scrumpets" — a cross between an oversize scone and a crumpet. Serves 6.

1 pint	Homemade Crème Fraîche (recipe follows)	250 mL
2 cups	*each* fresh strawberries, sliced, and fresh raspberries or blueberries	250 mL
2-3 tbsp.	sugar (more if needed)	30-45 mL
6	scrumpets	6
6 tbsp.	softened butter	90 mL
	fresh mint or strawberry leaves for garnish	

Prepare and chill the Homemade Crème Fraîche at least 24-48 hours before starting the shortcake. Mash about one-third of the sliced strawberries with the back of a spoon to a chunky purée. Combine with the raspberries (or blueberries) and remaining sliced strawberries, sprinkle with sugar to taste, and refrigerate 1-3 hours.

Heat the oven to 350°F (180°C). Place the scrumpets on a cookie sheet, and heat 5 minutes. Split open with a fork. Place one bottom half, split side up, on each dessert plate and butter each lightly with 1 tbsp. (15 mL) of the butter. Spoon over some berries and Crème Fraîche. Cover each with a scrumpet top, and cover with more cream and berries. Spoon any remaining berries around the base of each shortcake. Garnish with 1 or 2 whole berries and a mint or strawberry leaf. Serve at once.

HOMEMADE CRÈME FRAÎCHE

3 cups	whipping cream	750 mL
6 tbsp.	buttermilk	90 mL

Whisk together the cream and buttermilk, place in a glass jar, cover and let stand at warm room temperature 24-48 hours until thickened to the consistency of sour cream. Stir smooth and refrigerate until ready to use.

The Easy Gourmet features a photograph of this recipe on page 143.

CARIBBEAN FRUIT SALAD

Some desserts fall in and out of fashion over the years, but fresh fruit salads never lose their popularity. In this recipe the flavours of the Caribbean are brought to the lovely tropical fruits available in the produce department. Add a spiced syrup with a dash of rum, top with scoops of ice cream and you'll think you're on a tropical island. Serves 8.

2-3	medium oranges	2-3
1	lemon	1
1/3 cup	brown sugar	75 mL
1/4 tsp.	cinnamon	1 mL
pinch	nutmeg	pinch
2 tbsp.	dark rum *or*	30 mL
1 tsp.	imitation rum extract	5 mL
2 cups	fresh pineapple chunks	500 mL
1	mango, peeled and cut in thin strips	1
2	nectarines, sliced	2
2	bananas, peeled and sliced	2
1/2	cantaloupe, peeled, seeded and cut in chunks or slices	1/2
	coarsely grated fresh coconut to decorate (optional)	

Squeeze the juice from the oranges. Strain the juice into a measuring jug. You should have 1/2 cup (125 mL). Squeeze the juice from the lemon and add it to the orange juice. Add enough water to make 1 cup (250 mL). Pour the juice mixture into a small saucepan and stir in the sugar, cinnamon and nutmeg. Bring to a boil, then reduce the heat and simmer for 10 minutes. Remove from the heat and allow to cool. Add the rum or rum extract.

Place the prepared pineapple, mango, nectarines, bananas and melon in a serving bowl. Pour the cooled juice mixture over the fruit and stir lightly to mix. Cover and refrigerate until chilled. Sprinkle with grated coconut just before serving if desired.

SUMMER BERRY
ICE CREAM PIE

This dessert is spectacular to serve and a snap to prepare! Be easy on yourself — buy a frozen pie shell as the starter, pick up a quart of your favourite strawberry ice cream and a box of frozen raspberries, then follow these easy directions. Makes one 9 inch (23 cm) pie.

1 cup	fresh strawberries, sliced	250 mL
2-3 tbsp. + 1/3 cup	sugar	30-45 mL + 75mL
1	9 inch (23 cm) frozen pie shell, baked according to package directions until golden brown, cooled completely	1
1 quart	strawberry ice cream, slightly softened	1 L
1 cup	whipping cream	250 mL
2 tbsp.	icing sugar	30 mL
1 tsp.	pure vanilla extract	5 mL
1	9 oz. (300 g) package frozen raspberries	1

Toss the sliced strawberries with 2-3 tbsp. (30-45 mL) of the sugar. Place in the bottom of the baked pie shell. Freeze 20 minutes until firm. Top with softened ice cream, mounding slightly in the centre. Freeze immediately.

Whip the cream with the icing sugar and vanilla to slightly stiff peaks (do not beat dry). "Ice" the top of the pie completely with whipped cream, making swirls and peaks. Place it in the freezer at once and freeze 4-5 hours or overnight.

Meanwhile, prepare a raspberry sauce by thawing the raspberries and puréeing in a blender or food processor. Add up to 1/3 cup (75 mL) sugar, if needed, to taste. Heat in a small saucepan 3-4 minutes to dissolve the sugar. Cool and chill overnight.

To serve the pie, bring it to room temperature for 10 minutes before slicing into generous wedges. Drizzle each serving with a generous spoonful of chilled raspberry sauce. Enjoy!

GLAZED FRUIT FLAN

Sponge cake flans are available in the bakery or deli department. About 10 inches (25 cm) in diameter and ready to go, they are not only convenient but they are wonderful filled with sweet custard and topped with those fresh and fabulous summer fruits. Choose the fruit for colour and texture, then top it all with a thin glaze for a professional look. Serves 12-16.

3 tbsp.	sugar	45 mL
2 tbsp.	cornstarch	30 mL
1 cup	milk	250 mL
2	eggs, well beaten	2
1 tbsp.	Grand Marnier (optional)	15 mL
2 tsp.	vanilla	10 mL
1	prepared sponge cake flan shell	1
	fresh fruit	

Glaze:

2/3 cup	apricot jam	150 mL

In a medium saucepan, mix together the sugar and cornstarch. Stir in the milk and eggs. Bring to a boil, reduce the heat and cook gently, stirring, until the mixture coats a metal spoon and is slightly thickened. Add the Grand Marnier and vanilla. Cool slightly. Spoon into the flan shell.

Top the custard with a combination of strawberries, raspberries and blackberries, or try peaches and blueberries, or oranges and grapes, or various shades of plums.

To make the glaze, rub the apricot jam through a sieve into a saucepan and bring to a boil. Gently spoon or brush the hot jam over the fruit. Refrigerate until serving time.

CHERRY-KIWI MERINGUES

Here is the ultimate in summer desserts — a wonderfully creamy custard topped with perfect fresh cherries and kiwi fruit, all served up in meringue shells that come ready-made from the in-store bakery. In a word, mmmmmm! Serves 6.

1 1/2 tbsp.	all-purpose flour	20 mL
1 1/2 tbsp.	cornstarch	20 mL
1/3 cup	sugar	75 mL
1 cup	milk	250 mL
3	egg yolks	3
2 tbsp.	very soft butter	30 mL
1 tsp.	vanilla	5 mL
6	meringue shells	6
18	cherries, pitted	18
3	kiwi fruits, peeled and sliced	3
3 tbsp.	ground toasted hazelnuts	45 mL
4 tbsp.	whipping cream, whipped	60 mL

In a medium bowl, mix together the flour, cornstarch and sugar. Add enough of the milk, a spoonful at a time, to make a smooth paste. Add the remaining milk and pour the mixture into a medium saucepan. In a small bowl, beat the egg yolks lightly with a fork. Slowly heat the milk over low to medium heat, stirring constantly, until slightly thickened and creamy, about 10 minutes. Add some of the hot milk mixture to the beaten eggs, whisking rapidly. Return this mixture to the saucepan and cook a further 2 minutes to cook the egg, stirring constantly. Stir in the butter and vanilla.

Place a piece of plastic wrap on top of the custard to prevent a skin from forming. At serving time, spoon the custard into the meringue shells and decorate with the cherries and kiwi. Sprinkle each meringue with toasted hazelnuts and a dollop of freshly whipped cream.

INDEX

Updates on Volume One

Revisions to *The Easy Gourmet,* Volume One, *Entrées: The Main Event,* are as follows:

Old World Calves Liver with Bacon and Apples (p. 22): Use just enough cinnamon to sprinkle over the apples. Use 2 tsp. (10 mL) lemon juice and the grated rind of 1 lemon.

Southwest Short Ribs (p. 23): Use 2 tsp. (10 mL) salt.

Classic Meatballs Southern-Style (p. 29): Use 1 tsp. (5 mL) salt in the meat mixture.

Meatballs Stroganoff (p. 33): The first sentence of the directions should read: Combine the meat with the egg, bread crumbs, wheat germ, basil, pepper, 4 tbsp. (60 mL) of the soup, 4 tbsp. (60 mL) of the sour cream and 2 tbsp. (30 mL) of the parsley.

Italian Sausages with "Tri-Colore" Peppers (p. 37): Use salt to taste, 2 tsp. (10 mL) sugar, 1 tbsp. (15 mL) red wine vinegar, 2 tbsp. (30 mL) capers and 2 tbsp. (30 mL) minced fresh parsley.

Indonesian Nasi Goreng (p. 79): Use shelled fresh cooked shrimp.

Stuffed Turkey Roast (p. 91): Brown the roast for 10 minutes in the top third of a heated 375°F (160°C) oven.

Turkey Parmesan, Italian-Style (p. 97): Use 12 oz. (375 mL) marinara sauce.

Mussels Marinara (p. 123): Sauté half the garlic with the onion and use the other half in steaming the mussels. Garlic-lovers will want to double the amount of garlic called for.

Crispy Clam Fritters (p. 127): Use 1 pint (500 mL) shucked baby clams, 1 3/4 cups (425 mL) all-purpose flour, 1 tsp. (5 mL) salt, 1 tsp. (5 mL) paprika, 1 tbsp. (15 mL) baking powder, 1/2 tsp. (2 mL) sugar, and 1/4 tsp. (1 mL) each ground allspice, nutmeg and cracked black pepper.

Creole BBQ Shrimp, Cajun-Style (p. 135): Use 1 tbsp. (15 mL) paprika, 12 drops liquid hot pepper sauce, 2 tbsp. (30 mL) fresh lemon juice and the grated rind of 1 lemon. Delete the 1 tbsp. (15 mL) pepper.

Wraparound Prawns on Sweet and Sour Sauce (pp. 136-37): After preparing the sauce, broil the prawns 6 inches (15 cm) from the heat for 8 minutes or until the bacon is crisp and the prawns opaque. Turn once during the cooking time. Remove the sticks and place each serving of prawns on a bed of sauce. Sprinkle with parsley and serve.

Overnight Cheese Puff (p. 153): Use 1 1/2 tsp. (7 mL) salt.